Rise to the Occasion

Le bonheur est dans la cuisine...

Hedda et Chérif

Photograph by Les Hall

Rise to the Occasion

A French Food Experience

Hedda Gioia Dowd,
Cherif Brahmi,
and Celine Chick

Photography by Courtney Perry

Forewords by Edward Giobbi and Shirley O. Corriher

PELICAN PUBLISHING COMPANY

GRETNA 2011

*The word "Pelican" and the depiction of a pelican are
trademarks of Pelican Publishing Company, Inc., and are
registered in the U.S. Patent and Trademark Office.*

Library of Congress Cataloging-in-Publication Data

Dowd, Hedda Gioia.
  Rise to the occasion : a French food experience / Hedda Gioia Dowd, Cherif
Brahmi, and Celine Chick ; photography by Courtney Perry ; forewords by Edward
Giobbi and Shirley O. Corriher.
      p. cm.
  Includes bibliographical references and index.
  ISBN 978-1-58980-856-0 (hardcover : alk. paper) 1. Cooking, French. 2. Soufflés. 3.
Rise n°1 (Restaurant) 4. Entertaining. I. Brahmi, Cherif. II. Chick, Celine. III. Title.
  TX719.D665 2011
  641.8'2—dc22
                                        2010024108

Photograph of rise n°1 on front jacket by Les Hall

Printed in Singapore
Published by Pelican Publishing Company, Inc.
1000 Burmaster Street, Gretna, Louisiana 70053

Contents

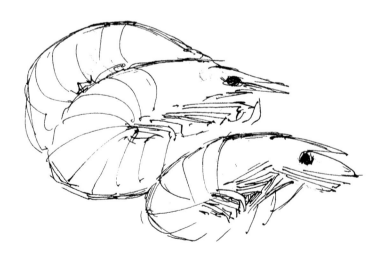

Foreword

Hedda Gioia Dowd is the most determined home cook I know. She has always been completely focused on cooking and the pleasures of dining.

Her enthusiasm for cooking has paid handsome dividends, as the owner of a successful restaurant and as a home cook.

Hedda's father was of Italian origin and her mother was of French origin. Can there be a better cooking heritage?

Chef Cherif Brahmi was a guest in our home one weekend. I immediately became aware that he was a talented chef in the French tradition. His passion for food was contagious.

I cannot imagine a better match than Hedda and Cherif. This book is a must for serious cooks and cookbook collectors.

Edward Giobbi

Acclaimed American painter and bestselling author of *Eat Right, Eat Well, The Italian Way* and *Italian Family Dining: Recipes, Menus, and Memories of Meals with a Great American Food Family*

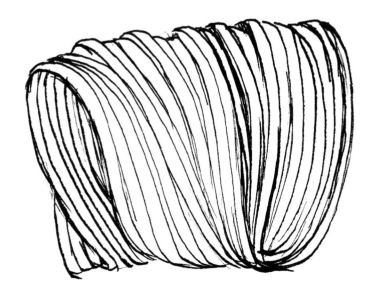

You will love this book. From rise n°1, the soufflé restaurant, owners Hedda Gioia Dowd and Chef Cherif Brahmi share treasures with you. Soufflés are a miracle of air and eggs—high and browned. And then, when you dip in, you are greeted by luscious, soft creaminess—the wonder and joy of soufflés! There are also beloved recipes of Hedda's childhood, with memories of her French mother and grandmother. Delightful dishes include Andrée's Orange Surprise—oranges hollowed, filled with sherbet and Grand Marnier-flavored whipped cream, and frozen with a secret piece of chocolate hidden in one orange.

In the Beef Volcano, Chef Cherif adds a warm, comfort-food touch to marvelous classic French boeuf bourguignon, with steaming, creamy mashed potatoes forming a volcano to cradle the bourguignon.

The photographs are inviting—from a speckled Araucana hen on her nest to escargots served in antique French escargot shells on fig leaves on an antique bread board.

The stories are engaging, from tales of famous French chefs to mysteries on Hedda's farm, such as how Ramon solved the problem of the missing eggs.

Rise to the Occasion is more than just recipes. It is like the joy of a soufflé itself—a wonderful, warm experience.

Shirley O. Corriher
Author of *CookWise* and *BakeWise*

From left to right: Escargot Soufflé, Ham and Cheese Soufflé, Cranberry Soufflé, Spinach Soufflé, Chocolate Soufflé, Violet Soufflé

Preface

Food is not only sustenance. Food is nurturing, soothing, and satisfying.

Hedda Gioia Dowd and Chef Cherif Brahmi, owners of rise n°1 in Dallas, Texas, have put food at the center of restaurant and family life. Preparing a delectable meal is first and foremost a way to seduce the epicurean in all of us, to titillate our senses, delight our palates with sheer pleasure, and make us feel whole again. Hedda firmly believes "it is in the sustenance of food that you develop your whole being."

Hedda grew up eating soufflés and remembers the excitement and mystery surrounding them. She loved peering into the oven window to see them rise. Hedda wanted to share the wonder and joy she experienced as a girl in her French mother's kitchen. Rise restaurant was born: part restaurant, part family tribute, part heritage, and part retail experience, but fully Hedda and Cherif's creation.

This book is a tribute to food, tradition, family, and good company.

Hedda Gioia Dowd

Oh ! l'amour d'une mère..
Amour que nul n'oublie..
Pain merveilleux
Q'un Dieu partage
et muliplie..
Table toujours servie
au paternel Foyer..
Chacun en a sa part
Et tous l'ont tout entier !.. Victor Hu

Acknowledgments

I would like to dedicate this book to my parents, Andrée and D. Frederick Gioia, who gave me a fire in my stomach from the moment I was born, and a daily journey through example.

For as long as I can remember, food has been the center of my universe. One of my earliest and fondest memories is climbing a cherry tree in my grandparents' grove in France, sitting on a branch, picking my first pair of ruby earrings—red cherries— and placing them ever so carefully around each one of my ears. I moved my head from side to side just to feel the heaviness of the fruit against my skin. As I climbed down the tree to show them off to my family, I wondered how long they would last before I would devour them and all I had gathered in my pockets.

And so began my love affair with food and the path it took me on.

We are blessed in this life to enter a home with food covering the table and to fill our stomachs each and every day. I realize how many of us in the world will never know this feeling.

Daily, my senses were filled with the aromas and sounds of cooking by a master chef, my French mother. She brought food from her soul and heart to the table, and each day our family gathered to share our thoughts, trials, and pleasures over the most amazing meals.

I am certain that seeing, at my young age, her constantly cooking and the joy it brought her altered my life.

I never imagined that my life could revolve around what I prepare and eat three times a day, but it does and should. Great purpose and thought should go into that which fuels us each day.

I never want to miss a meal, and should it ever be my last, I want it to be shared and memorable.

I want to give thanks for how the ink got on these pages. No one does anything well alone. . . .

I am fortunate to have met my chef partner, Cherif Brahmi, in Dallas in 1978. If it weren't for his culinary skills, craft, and infinite patience with me, the soufflés at rise would never have been "born." Our shared recipe book would not be here and I could not have become a restaurateur.

Thanks to my siblings, Eric, Germaine, and Dominique, who grew up sharing and witnessing this lifelong obsession of mine. They will never realize how appreciative I am of them. No one but a sibling would tolerate listening to so much talk about food.

Thanks to my late husband, Hector P. "Jack" Dowd, who always said, "Don't sweat the mule going blind. . . . Just load the wagon!"

Thanks to André, my son. Before we opened, he hand-placed ever so carefully all 262 recycled wine bottles on our antique wine-drying-rack chandelier and then over months spent infinite hours in conversation over public-relations strategies that have proven invaluable.

Thanks to the Gioia, Dowd, Horner, Scaggs, Gillikin, Denegre, and Scotti families and my supportive friends. "We" is the operative word!

Cherif and I are fortunate to have a dedicated team beside us. So we acknowledge you:

Our coauthor Celine Chick. Her research and dedication are beyond all expectations. We are all the beneficiaries.

Our photographer, Courtney Perry. The photographs speak for themselves.

Our management at rise—Tara Brahmi, Richard Bertschi, James Dembecki, and Jesus Franco.

And our committed staff at rise and honored guests.

Merci!

Hedda

Staff with Pres. George W. Bush (back row, center) and Laura Bush and Hedda Dowd (front row, right)

First and foremost, this book is a tribute to my mother, Sadia, and my father, Moussa. I would also like to extend my gratitude to my brothers and sisters, Said, Rabah, Hadjila, Belkacem, Kader, Louisa, and Boalem, for always giving me the wisdom and resolve to reach for my goals. I would like to thank my children, Alisha, Preston, and Tara, and their mother, Darlene, for all their encouragement over my years in the restaurant business. Furthermore, I would like to thank all the people who helped me in any shape or form to excel as an individual and allowed me to follow my career as a chef.

My curiosity for cooking came not only from watching my mother cook but also through all the exquisite dishes that left me in awe. My mother was always cheerful and looked forward to cooking for and nourishing our family. Through my mother's love and respect for cooking, my own interest to cook was born. I stumbled into cooking school by chance, but ever since the day I entered that classroom in 1970, I made cooking my life and passion.

Since 1975, I have cooked professionally across Europe and the United States. Through my experience and exposure to the cooking world, I have cooked many types of cuisine under many legendary mentors. Jean Lafont, Gilbert Drouelle, and Albert Clément, thank you for sharing your enthusiasm, passion, and knowledge with me.

I now own my own restaurant, rise, with Hedda Gioia Dowd, my business partner and all-around woman extraordinaire, who never took no for an answer when I didn't believe that the concept of a soufflé restaurant could be as successful as it has been. Thank you, Hedda, for your continued perseverance and inspiring spirit and for making me a believer in your dreams.

In short, this road has not been an easy one. Every day brings a new and exciting challenge, with many unexpected turns. I thank each and every person I have encountered for his or her efforts, support, and will to work under my leadership as a chef. You know who you are, and if you do not, come find me!

Let's rise!

Cherif

Top: Cherif (rear), Jean Troisgros, Pierre Troisgros, and Jean Lafont. Middle left: Lafont and Cherif with 16 pounds of French truffles at Old Warsaw in Dallas. Middle right: Carl DiCristofalo, Paul Bocuse, Mario Messina, and Cherif in Dallas. Bottom: Cherif.

Cherif's mother, Sadia Brahmi

Rise to the Occasion

1
The Ritual of Eating

The sound of an eggshell cracking against a silver bowl and a whisk dipping into the pastel-yellow liquid, spinning relentlessly against the sides of the bowl until it rests amidst the blended mixture, could very well conjure up three images: your mother and you wearing aprons on Sunday afternoon and baking goods, or your grandmother in the kitchen of her country home, or thirdly and sadly, you watching a rerun of a cooking show, sleep deprived and wishing that for just a moment you could recreate the simple gesture of cracking an egg and enjoy cooking.

Life as we know it in the United States is fast. We can drive through and pick up a hamburger, salad, brownie, and coffee without leaving the comfort of our car seat. We can make a business transaction from our phone while waiting in line at the grocery store, and we can download and upload anything and everything with the touch of a button.

What if we could just press the "pause" button in our lives?

On the other side of the Atlantic, in some remote villages in France, life follows a different rhythm. People wake up with the cackle of a hen at dawn and meander through the streets on their red bicycles or blue cars to the *boulangerie*, where they pick up a freshly baked baguette or warm croissant. They go to work, and during their lunch break, they take the time to saddle back up on their bicycles or buckle up in their automobile and head home to have a copious meal with their families or friends.

Eating is a communal and simple act. The food need not be sophisticated or fussy, but rather rustic and hearty. Eating becomes a pleasure and not a rushed necessity.

At rise, eating takes on a more spiritual dimension. People in the dining room feel a true connection between the food they are eating and the atmosphere they are immersed in. It is as though time has stopped, so that nothing can come between your meal and your enjoyment of it. Until you leave the restaurant through its antique temple double doors, you feel enveloped in warmth and comfort. Your dining experience ends with a quote, which a hostess hands you on your way out—a thought for the day. The experience is so unique that one guest, after receiving his quote of the day, exclaimed, "Rise is a massage for the soul!" Eating at rise is more than a ritual; it is a means to open up your soul to an enchanting and uplifting experience that will leave you wanting more. As another guest explained, "I'm feeding my soul as well as my body." Nourishment for the soul comes from a combination of good food, good company, and a welcoming environment.

A few of our favorite quotes from the quote wheel:

"The sun, with all those planets revolving around it and dependent on it, can still ripen a bunch of grapes as if it had nothing else in the universe to do."

Galileo

"The only thing that will make a soufflé fall is if it knows you are afraid of it."

James Beard

"You will wait on your soufflé but your soufflé will not wait on you!"

Anonymous

Like alchemists transforming base metals into gold, Cherif and Hedda spend time preparing food until it becomes so good

Cherif grating salt

it is golden. In order to fully appreciate the food they prepare, they return to a way of preparing and eating that is informed by tradition while being respectful of nature.

Part of eating involves tradition. Oftentimes, we create our own rituals and traditions depending on our availability. We tell family members when we would like to get together and eat as a family. Thanksgiving is an American tradition, which we take pride in. Most of us cook with family and friends to create a satisfying meal that is then shared and enjoyed. The tradition of Thanksgiving brings us closer together, because all households either cook or order the same meal.

When Cherif visits relatives in France, he partakes in the tradition of the Sunday meal at his parents' house. Just like when he was growing up, the whole family knows that they can come over every Sunday to join in a meal. His mother made couscous every Sunday, using vegetables from her garden. Cherif confesses that is one of the traditions he misses the most while living in America. The good thing about France is that most of the shops and businesses are closed on Sunday, so very few people are working. Spending time with family and friends is everything. In America, because we work so much, we have developed a bit of a "calendar culture." We constantly refer back to our calendars to see when we can fit someone into our schedule, even if that person happens to be family.

Henri IV, king of France in the sixteenth century, decreed that all workers should be entitled to a *poule au pot,* a chicken in every pot. This dish went on to become the national dish of France. Still today, many people in France eat a chicken on Sundays in observance of this centuries-old tradition.

When signing the Public Broadcasting Act of 1967, Pres. Lyndon B. Johnson famously quoted Henry IV: "It announces to the world that our nation wants more than just material wealth; our nation wants more than a 'chicken in every pot.' We in America have an appetite for excellence, too."

Had President Johnson already forgotten that we in America already have more than the simple chicken in the pot? We have the twelve-pound Thanksgiving turkey. That is an American achievement!

2

Eating Healthy

We all strive for balance in our lives, whether it is the balance between work and children or love and family. But the balance we should seek out first, as it appears to be the most important, is the balance between a healthy mind and a healthy body. Juvenal, the Roman poet, introduced the idea of *mens sana in corpore sano* (a healthy mind in a healthy body) as part of a long list of what people should desire in life. Oftentimes, we forget that health should always be the first priority in life. Without health, we have nothing. With it, we have possibilities and opportunities.

A healthy mind often comes from having a healthy body. We can attain a healthy body through proper nutrition and exercise, as advocated in numerous health magazines. Eating healthily does not equate to dieting. Eating healthily is enjoyable and easy to do. Eggs are Hedda's favorite healthy ingredients because they are the most complete whole food you can live on. She explains, "Eggs and water are all you need. It might get boring, but you have everything you need." Furthermore, eggs are versatile and can be used to make anything from a savory dish to a sweet dish. Eggs are the focal ingredients at rise, because they are healthy and the main component of soufflés. Eggs are nutritious all around. They are a great source of protein, vitamin A, vitamin D, and folic acid. They contain choline, which can help prevent Alzheimer's; and the lutein in the yolks can lend a hand in preventing macular degeneration, an eye disease.

Rebecca Wright, a registered dietitian with the Cancer Treatment Centers of America, came to rise for a meal and was pleasantly surprised with the diversity on the menu. She began to tell Hedda about the difficulties cancer patients encounter with chewing foods. Egg protein is a good, easy-to-digest protein and gentle on damaged tissue. It is an ideal food for cancer patients who are in need of supplemental protein. Soufflés are an original and satisfying way of utilizing egg protein for cancer patients, as soft foods tend to lack variety.

As we have often heard, "the body is a temple." This signifies that, like a religious temple, it must be respected and cared for. We must be mindful of what we place in our bodies. If we solely ingest chemical-laden foods, we feel the effects on our body. We might feel lethargic or experience unusual headaches. Eating whole foods is the answer to maintaining a healthy body.

Cooking is an art form. A good home cook, like an artist, can be talented without any training. To cook a good meal, if you are inexperienced in the kitchen, you must arm yourself with two very important qualities: patience and a sense of humor. The first time Hedda made bread, she alleged it was so hard it could have been used as a weapon. She laughed about it but tried again until she could turn it into the desired consistency. As Hedda explains, to be a good cook, "you need to get in the kitchen."

"Hedda cooking," as Cherif has come to call it, takes on a life of its own. To truly understand her take on healthy cooking, you must make the pilgrimage to her farm in Hunt County, Texas. Cows roam freely amongst donkeys, sheep, ducks, and geese, which Hedda says invited themselves and never left. Time here has stopped, and if it weren't for the Texas summer heat, you would think you were in Provence.

Hedda's cooking is original. She has outfitted her fireplace with a removable grill/grate. The fireplace also houses an eighteenth-century French *tournebroche,*[1] which took three years and many savvy people to restore. She often roasts duck and chicken on her *tournebroche,* accompanied by fruits and vegetables, which she cooks on her grate with her secret seasonings. "Fruits can

taste a certain way when they are picked from a bush or a tree, but once you cook them, they can taste entirely different," she explains. Hedda doesn't believe in conventional side dishes such as potatoes or rice when she cooks. She goes to the market to buy an assortment of colorful fruit and vegetables, and all this produce becomes an integral part of the feast. Cherif reveals that in all his years of cooking, he has never come across anything like Hedda prepares. She pours all her beliefs into these dishes cooked over open fires. They are healthy and simple and, most of all, they engage our curiosity.

Hedda uses a bunch of basil as a brush to spread an olive-oil mixture onto most any fowl, then adds grilled figs, grapes, and cherries, and the dish ends up looking like a version of a "fruit face" painting by Giuseppe Arcimboldo.[2] It is at this point that you truly understand that cooking is an art form, whether you are a trained chef or a novice in the kitchen.

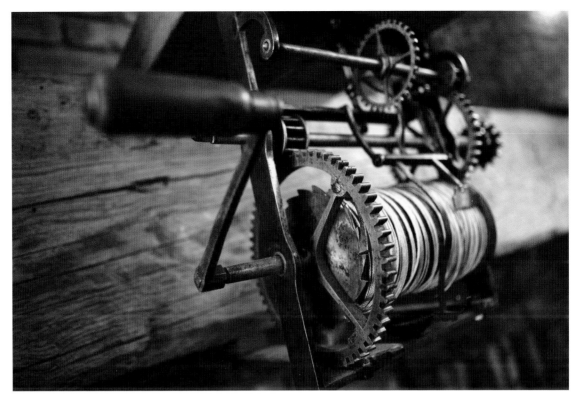

Hedda's tournebroche

Hens on the tournebroche

Eggs and Soldiers

Eggs and Soldiers

Eggs and soldiers are a playful and healthy meal for children of all ages.

Yields 6 servings

Water
6 eggs
12 slices bread, toasted
Salt to taste
Pepper to taste

Fill a medium saucepan with enough water to cover eggs. Bring the water to a simmer and add the eggs.

Cook for 4-6 minutes, depending on how runny you like your eggs.

Cut the top part of the shell off each egg.

Cut toasts into 1" vertical slices, for dipping in the eggs.

Season eggs with salt and pepper. Arrange the bread around each egg.

Hay-Roasted Duck

Hay-Roasted Duck

Hedda got the idea for this dish from roasting a lamb on hay. The hay gives the ducks a wonderful flavor and aroma.

Yields 4-6 servings

1 1,500-pound bale of hay
2 cups water
2 whole ducks, cleaned and rinsed inside and out, patted dry
Salt to taste
Pepper to taste

Preheat oven to 375 degrees.

Cover the base of a 12"x16" pan with 1 pound hay.

Donate remaining 1,499 pounds hay to a local stable or dairy farm.

Add water to hay in pan.

With a fork, prick or score ducks all over. Bend wings backwards.

Generously sprinkle with salt and pepper inside and out.

Place ducks on hay, breast side down.

Roast in oven for about 30 minutes.

Turn ducks over and roast for another 30 minutes, or until the internal temperature of each duck reads 160 degrees on a meat thermometer and the ducks' skin is golden brown.

Tip: Replace the hay with a medley of herbs if you have no access to hay. Herb suggestions: rosemary, mint, sage, oregano, and lavender.

Gazpacho

Gazpacho

Rise guests clamor for this healthy and low-calorie soup. The chipotle paste gives this simple recipe a little heat.

Yields 4-6 servings

1 pound roma tomatoes, quartered and cored
1 pound cucumber, peeled and diced
1 red bell pepper, chopped
2 cups V8 juice
1 cup chopped yellow onion
4 tablespoons apple cider vinegar
1 tablespoon olive oil
½ teaspoon chipotle paste
Salt to taste
Pepper to taste
1 bunch chives, chopped (optional)
Cucumbers and tomatoes, diced (optional)

Place tomatoes, cucumber, bell pepper, V8, onion, vinegar, olive oil, chipotle paste, salt, and pepper in a food processor.

Blend until smooth.

Serve chilled. Garnish with chives, cucumbers, and tomatoes if desired.

Tip: Gazpacho tastes best when made the same day as serving.

Salmon Rillettes

Salmon Rillettes

This is an easy and flavorful appetizer. Buy your favorite fresh salmon at a local fish market.

Yields 4-6 servings

> 4 ounces fresh, skinless salmon
> 1 tablespoon olive oil
> Salt to taste
> Pepper to taste
> 1 Boursin cheese (5.2 ounces)
> 2 tablespoons mayonnaise
> Crostini (toasted baguette slices)

Preheat oven to 450 degrees.

Coat salmon with olive oil and season with salt and pepper.

Place salmon on a parchment-lined baking sheet.

Bake for 12-15 minutes until cooked through. Remove from oven and refrigerate.

When salmon is chilled, place in mortar. Using pestle, blend with Boursin and mayonnaise until smooth.

Serve with crostini.

Steak Tartare

Steak Tartare

Steak tartare can be made with ground or chopped raw beef. Be sure to acquire your meat from a good source, to avoid any risk associated with eating uncooked meats.

Yields 4-6 servings

12 ounces beef tenderloin, ground or chopped
2 egg yolks
⅓ cup chopped red onion
⅓ cup chopped cornichons
⅓ cup chopped capers
⅓ cup finely chopped parsley
2 tablespoons brandy (optional)
1½ tablespoons Dijon mustard
1 tablespoon ketchup
1 tablespoon olive oil
1 teaspoon Worcestershire sauce
1 teaspoon Tabasco sauce
2 mini baguettes, toasted

Using a wooden spoon or spatula, combine the meat with egg yolks, red onion, cornichons, capers, parsley, brandy, mustard, ketchup, olive oil, Worcestershire sauce, and Tabasco.

Serve with toasted baguettes.

Tip: Ketchup gives the meat a nice red color. Pommes frites may be served in place of the baguettes.

3

The Road Less Traveled

Cherif became a chef by accident. When he was sick on the day of his accounting entrance exam, he was told about a new program in his school dedicated to cooking. Cherif took to it like a duck to water. He loved that at the end of his cooking classes, he could enjoy the fruits of his labor. He went on to get a degree, which allowed him to cook in a professional setting. Every weekend, as part of the school curriculum, he would apprentice at different restaurants in Lyon, one of France's culinary capitals. During these weekends, Cherif experienced real-world cooking, in kitchens where adapting to your chef and environment were a must if you wanted to learn. Through these apprenticeships, he garnered many useful techniques and furthered his knowledge of food.

One particular chef at a *relais routier*[1] in Lyon left a lasting impression on Cherif. Cherif remembers his *gratin dauphinois*,[2] *moules marinières*,[3] and coffee ice cream as simply incredible. The quality of the ingredients and the way they were prepared were unlike anything he had seen in his schooling.

After school ended, Cherif decided to work as a seasonal chef, alternating between summers at the beach and winters in the mountains of France. In Val D'Isere,[4] he worked as a server for part of the season. Cherif learned both sides of the business and found a new appreciation and respect for waiters. He understood the dynamics between a chef and his wait staff and learned how to deal with delays by sending out sorbet between courses.

Cherif later moved to Paris and worked at a prestigious hotel, the PLM Saint Jacques. It was the first hotel of its kind, with a business-chic approach, and counted French celebrities such as Serge Gainsbourg and Jacques Dutronc among its guests. The hotel boasted three restaurants, 800 rooms, and banquet rooms. Cherif rotated among the three restaurants, seamlessly alternating from the sauce station to the dessert station. He claims that this is where he learned to make a good omelette, the skill that best demonstrates whether a chef is worthy of being in a kitchen. Cherif elaborates, "A good chef can make a good omelette. The secret is in the technique. You need a touch of butter, a touch of olive oil, and the butter must be just the right temperature so the omelette doesn't stick to the pan."

A general manager at the hotel helped Cherif with his next step: coming to Dallas. Cherif was hired to work there under Chef Jean Lafont at the Oz Club. This upscale restaurant hosted many French chef masters for private membership dinners, such as Pierre Laporte, Alain Chapel, and the Troisgros brothers. Cherif recognizes that he would never have had the opportunity to work with such culinary talent back in France. After two years as a saucier, Cherif took the helm as the head chef. He was only twenty-two years old.

"You wake up very quickly" when you run a kitchen, says Cherif. The pressures, worries, and responsibilities are immense.

For seven years Cherif served under Jean Lafont as the head chef at Dallas's Old Warsaw, where he could let his imagination run wild to invent dishes. His primary inspiration came from the *Larousse Gastronomique*, the French encyclopedia of gastronomy. "Anything we saw, if it could be done, we did it," he recalls. Cherif remembers his time at the Old Warsaw as the ultimate culinary experience. Lafont once made a *poularde en vessie*,[5] stuffed with truffle and foie gras.[6] Cherif says it was unbelievable—it took all day to make, and the bladder looked like a balloon. Lafont then poked it to release the air and sliced it up. "The flavor was just *incroyable* [incredible]," Cherif declares.

Hedda, originally from Memphis, Tennessee, began her career

in retail, where she met her husband. She later answered her food calling, working for a French company that supplied Dallas hotels and restaurants with cheese, truffles, and fish flown in from Paris. She also worked at Sur La Table, a cooking store, in their cooking-class division, where she broadened her food knowledge. During a class, a Vietnamese chef squatted on the floor with a mortar and pestle and started pounding food with an intense focus. Hedda immediately felt a connection, although she did not know the food. Through this woman's passion, and her deep involvement with the dish, she felt that she understood everything she needed to about this foreign food. Her father always told her as a girl that she was meant to work with food.

In 1978, Cherif was working for Phil Vaccaro (cousin of *Midnight Cowboy* actress Brenda Vaccaro), who owned many prestigious restaurants in Dallas. A purchasing agent for Vaccaro's restaurants was a mutual friend of Cherif and Hedda and introduced them.

When Hedda first approached Cherif about the concept for rise, he was skeptical. "I liked the idea [of a soufflé restaurant] but I wasn't really convinced. Hedda kept coming back to convince me it could work. I knew this was something no one had ever done before." After paying Chef Brahmi many visits, Hedda finally managed to convince him of the viability of her project. She wanted Cherif to do what he did best—helm the kitchen and create delectable soufflés. "You make soufflés, and I will take care of everything else," she told him.

When they opened the restaurant on January 15, 2008, the soufflé was perceived as a food for women. As Hedda notes, "It takes a real man to eat a soufflé." Cherif and Hedda added crabmeat and lobster to the mix, and soon men started coming through the doors, even booking business lunches at rise. Hedda exclaims, "I can't believe how many men were eating violet soufflés!"

Cherif advised Hedda to add steak and tuna to the menu as well. They soon realized, however, that they didn't sell many steaks. The soufflé, as Hedda had first dreamed, would be the star of the menu.

Socrates once said, "I know that I am intelligent, because I know that I know nothing." We never finish learning; we are always students. Cherif recognizes this truth: "I learn from every place I work. The day you think that you know it all, your career ends. You learn from your employees and guests too."

One day, a salesman came to rise and looked over the menu. He asked Cherif why a French-inspired restaurant was not serving escargot. Cherif thought this was a very good point and later added escargot soufflés to the menu.

Cooking is all about timing. Cherif calls it "knowing when." For example, you need to know when the pan is just the right temperature. If it is too hot, you will most likely burn the dish, and if it isn't hot enough, you might end up with another kind of disaster. "It's all timing. That's it!" he insists.

French cooking, as many have come to embrace, utilizes the best ingredients. Some of them, such as milk, cream, and butter, may seem heavy, but they are the foundation of French cooking. Butter, as Cherif indicates, has no substitute. He challenges, "When you make sauces, are you going to make a hollandaise with egg yolk and *olive oil?* I don't think so!" But what about those of us who fear for our hips if we consume milk, cream, or butter? Well, just take one look at French women . . . they enjoy life's simple pleasures in moderation. A little butter goes a long way.

If a professional chef such as Cherif could give advice to any home cook, he would encourage them not to be afraid to try something new. Food should not be intimidating. If you follow a set of directions and ideas, you will be successful. You just need to be willing. Hedda recommends, "Keep your food simple, and be true to how it is. You will be a fine cook."

Cherif creates recipes for soufflés, then wants to improve them constantly. Hedda remembers that the first time she had his chestnut soufflé, she thought it was magical, but Cherif told her there was room for improvement. Cherif is very methodical and a perfectionist; he will not stop until he reaches the perfection he envisions. But as Hedda says, "He's just got it! I think he is so humble that he will never admit he is so talented."

Guests get in touch with their emotions at rise, because they feel they are in their own home. An enthusiastic guest revealed she would someday like to have her ashes scattered at rise.

The more you involve your community, the more your concept will grow. Rise is deeply rooted in the community. Hedda and Cherif both believe that they serve their community and their community, in turn, helps them. Brookhaven College has worked with rise since its inception. Students in the ceramics department have helped create beautiful plates; *chocolat chaud*[7] cups, which are now used to serve the popular marshmallow soup; and a custom-ordered ramekin plate, which Cherif devised. The ramekin plate

was a "blend of creativity and need coming together," explains Hedda. The students are of all ages. They went to the school of life; therefore, their work is infused with great feeling and dedication.

Rise offers Antique Harvest, an online import business of antique linens, silver flatware, and cooking utensils collected from French chateaux, farmhouses, and *manoirs*[8] since 1995. Everything you can see or touch at rise is for sale, from the forest of trees close to the kitchen and the salt and pepper frogs to the books in the library. After eating dinner on an 18th-century school desk, a guest decided to purchase it to recreate the rise experience at her school.

Cherif and Hedda truly take pride in every step of the process at rise. They feel inspired and uplifted along the way by the people they encounter. "Having creative souls around you makes the process of opening the door worth it. You don't need reviews. You need people eating," insists Hedda.

To be in the restaurant business, as Hedda puts it, "You need to be passionate and you need to make it seamless." Running a restaurant is intense, because the day starts hours before the first guest comes in and ends hours after the last guest leaves. You have to be willing to give a lot of yourself in order to create a nurturing environment for your guests.

Having supportive people around you is invaluable as well.

One evening Hedda received a call from Celine, who said, "I have a package for you that is perishable. May I drop it off at rise?"

Hedda had just left the restaurant, as her son was going off to college and she wanted to cook a last meal for him. She was busy at home, immersed in the pleasures of cooking with Noilly Prat (dry vermouth) in one hand and a stirring spoon in the other. Hedda already had a call that a special dignitary was arriving at rise, so she told Celine she could meet her there briefly.

When Hedda arrived, Celine was waiting. Celine handed her a gift that may not bring tears to the eyes of a clotheshorse, but it pierced Hedda's heart. Celine had flown in fresh abalone in their shells as a treat to thank Hedda for a day at her farm!

In the midst of the busy restaurant, Hedda stood completely still within herself, absorbed in this magical moment of pure thoughtfulness, the sharing of a rare and beautiful gift given by one to another—simple, pure, and encompassing. After composing herself, Hedda listened to Celine's story about the abalone man. Then she raced home to learn how to delight in such a treat and to share this bounty and celebrate the rest of the evening.

Hedda and Cherif are so grateful to Celine for many reasons, but especially for joining them in writing this book. Merci!

Gratin Dauphinois

Gratin Dauphinois

Gratin dauphinois *is a popular potato dish from the Dauphine region of France. Potatoes are baked in a shallow dish with a golden crust of breadcrumbs or cheese. Gratin dauphinois is a good side for most meat or poultry dishes, such as Hay-Roasted Duck (see index). This is Cherif's preferred recipe of the traditional gratin dauphinois he made while training as a chef in Lyon, France.*

Yields 4-6 servings

> 2 tablespoons butter, divided
> 1 chopped teaspoon garlic
> 2 cups whole milk
> 2 pounds Idaho potatoes, peeled and sliced into
>   ⅛"-thick slices
> Salt to taste
> White Pepper to taste
> ½ teaspoon nutmeg
> 1 cup heavy whipping cream
> 5 tablespoons shaved good imported Parmesan

Preheat oven to 350 degrees.

Grease a 10"x10"x2" baking dish with 1 tablespoon softened butter. Pat garlic onto sides and bottom of dish.

In a large pot, heat the milk over low heat. When it is heated, add the potatoes. Add salt, pepper, and nutmeg.

Cook the potatoes on low heat, stirring often so the milk doesn't scald. After about 10 minutes, when a knife can easily go through the potatoes, remove them from the pot with a slotted spoon. The potatoes should have absorbed a lot of the liquid, but discard the rest of the liquid in the pot.

Evenly layer the potatoes in the buttered dish. Pour heavy cream over potatoes. Sprinkle the Parmesan evenly over the potatoes. Dot the potatoes with the remaining butter. Bake in the oven for 20-25 minutes until the top is golden brown.

Tip: As soon as you peel the potatoes, have the milk heated and ready to go. Potatoes will brown if left sitting out for too long.

4

All About Soufflés

A soufflé is an airy, fluffy, and light baked dish made from an egg-yolk base, egg whites, and other ingredients. The word "soufflé" is the past participle of the French verb *souffler,* which means to blow or fluff up. A soufflé can be served as a savory dish or sweet dessert. It gets its lift from the egg whites. Heat makes the egg whites in the soufflé expand, and exposure to cold air will make a soufflé deflate.

Typically, a savory soufflé consists of three different parts:

- A Mornay base, which is a béchamel sauce with egg yolk and cheese
- Egg whites beaten to peaks
- Savory flavoring ingredients (cheese, spinach puree, mushrooms, etc.)

A sweet soufflé consists of three parts:

- A pastry cream
- Egg whites beaten to peaks
- Sweet flavoring ingredients (chocolate, cranberries, strawberries, etc.)

Soufflés are a French invention dating back to the eighteenth century. They were first mentioned in Vincent La Chapelle's *Le Cuisinier Moderne* (*The Modern Cook)* in 1735. La Chapelle was a French chef to such dignitaries as Madame de Pompadour, the Earl of Chesterfield, and King Louis XV.

In England, the word *soufflé* first appeared in chef Louis Eustache Ude's cookbook, *The French Cook,* which was released in 1813. Ude apprenticed under his father for King Louis XVI and worked for Napoleon's mother, Princess Maria-Letizia, as a maitre d'hôtel for two years. He then left for England, where he worked for Earl Sefton and the Duke of York.

Below is one of La Chapelle's soufflé recipes from *Le Cuisinier Moderne.*

Timbales[1] of Cream.

You will have a good pastry cream, bitter almond biscuits, candied lemon peel, orange flower; add to these egg whites whipped into snow. You will have little timbale dishes greased with good fresh butter; you powder them with bread crumbs; then you fill them with your cream, and cook them in the oven. When they are done, turn them out and serve as a small hot entremet.[2]

A light, billowy, and fluffy omelette soufflé[3] similar to La Chapelle's original interpretation can be found today at La Mère Poulard, a hotel and restaurant in Mont Saint Michel, France, that dates back to 1879. These omelettes are still made to order in hammered copper bowls over open fires of oak wood. On a cool evening, after ambling through the streets of Mont Saint Michel, guests at La Mère Poulard will find the warmth and comfort they seek with an omelette they will forever engrave in their mind's palate.

Antonin Careme, known as one of the first celebrity chefs and creator of the standard chefs' hat, the toque, helped popularize the soufflé in the nineteenth century by calling it "the queen of hot pastries."

As Eliza Leslie points out in her 1851 book *Directions for Cookery,* if you can't make a soufflé yourself, hire a French chef to make it for you. "If you live in a large town, the safest way of avoiding

Buttering the ramekin

Coating the ramekin

Garnishing the soufflé

a failure in an omelette soufflé is to hire a French cook to come to your kitchen with his own utensils and ingredients, and make and bake it himself, while the first part of the dinner is progressing in the dining room."

If you happen to visit or live in Dallas, rise has delicious soufflés for you.

Fun fact: If you add fifteen times more flour to a basic soufflé recipe, you will have made a sponge cake.

Cherif's Conseils Pratiques for Soufflé Making

- Think ahead when making a soufflé. The soufflé base or Mornay can be made the day before and refrigerated.
- Keep the base warm. The flavoring ingredients must be combined with the soufflé base and warmed when mixed with the egg whites.
- The more soufflés you make, the more talented you will become. Soufflés are an art form.

Shirley Corriher's Tricks of the Trade

Shirley Corriher, biochemist and bestselling author of *BakeWise* and *CookWise*, offers these tricks of the trade.

Fresh eggs help make a more stable base for soufflés.

A warm base will give you a head start on the soufflé rising.

Insert a baking stone in the oven to place the soufflé ramekin on. This is one of Shirley's favorite tricks. She preheats the oven to about 50 degrees warmer than you would for a typical soufflé recipe and places the stone in the oven. She then reduces the heat to what the soufflé recipe requires and places the soufflé on top of the stone. In the oven there is a constant battle between the heat from the top, which helps form the crust but also holds a product down, and the heat from the bottom, which helps the product rise. The heat from the stone underneath will help your soufflé to rise.

Shirley's next trick is "the three-bowl method." In one bowl she places the yolks, in another the whites that are sometimes mixed with broken yolks, and in the third the perfectly white egg whites. The contents of the mixed bowl are discarded.

Beating an egg is like cooking it, she warns. For a soufflé, you want the whites to expand, but you don't want to overbeat them. If you do, the proteins from the egg will tighten around the air bubbles and will no longer expand.

Tara's Escargot Soufflé

Tara's Escargot Soufflé

Tara, Cherif's daughter, has become an authority on good escargot soufflés. This cloudlike goat-cheese soufflé with basil pesto is a real jewel to serve guests. Note that escargot soufflé dishes are different from regular ramekins; they have several compartments.

Yields 8-10 individual soufflés

BASIL PESTO

¼ pound fresh basil
1 tablespoon pecan pieces, toasted
1 teaspoon chopped garlic
¼ cup fresh parsley, washed with stems removed
½ tablespoon lemon juice
Salt to taste
Pepper to taste
1 tablespoon grated Parmesan
1 cup olive oil

Preheat oven to 375 degrees.

For the basil pesto, combine the basil, pecans, garlic, parsley, lemon juice, salt, pepper, and Parmesan in the bowl of an electric mixer. Slowly pour in olive oil to blend into an even paste. Set aside.

ESCARGOTS

1 can (1 pound) extra large snails
4 ounces butter
1 cup chopped shallots
½ cup garlic, chopped
4-5 thyme sprigs
2 small bay leaves
Salt to taste
Pepper to taste

For the escargots preparation, rinse and drain snails. In a large pot, heat butter on medium heat. Add shallots, garlic, thyme, and bay leaves, and cook until translucent. Add snails. Cook for 5 minutes. Season with salt and pepper. Arrange 1-2 cooked escargots per compartment of the soufflé dish.

ROUX

2 ounces butter
½ cup white flour

To make the roux, melt butter in a large pot over medium heat. Add flour and stir. Reduce heat to low. Cook for 2-3 minutes. Remove from heat to cool down.

SOUFFLE BASE

2 cups whole milk
½ teaspoon salt
½ teaspoon white pepper
½ teaspoon nutmeg
½ cup grated Swiss cheese
¼ cup grated Parmesan
3 egg yolks
10 ounces goat cheese
18 egg whites

For the soufflé base, in a different saucepan, bring milk to a boil. Add salt, white pepper, and nutmeg.

Pour hot milk slowly into the roux. Bring back to a boil, while stirring constantly, for about 2 minutes. Turn off the heat and keep stirring until the mixture thickens. Add the Swiss cheese, Parmesan, and the egg yolks, and stir. Add the goat cheese.

In the bowl of an electric mixer, beat the egg whites to soft peaks. The egg whites must have risen to peaks before you can combine them with the goat-cheese soufflé base.

Add the warm soufflé base to the egg whites in mixer; stir.

Pour 1 ice-cream scoop of soufflé base into each escargot compartment.

Place soufflés on lowest rack of oven. Leave 6-8″ space above the dish to allow soufflés to rise. Bake for 20-25 minutes. Top of soufflés should be browned.

Drizzle basil pesto on top of the soufflés before serving.

Tip: Use the leftover egg yolks to make crème anglaise (see next recipe).

Cranberry Soufflés with Crème Anglaise

These are a fall favorite at rise! Crème anglaise is the ideal sauce for berry-flavored desserts.

Yields 4 individual soufflés

½ cup butter
¼ cup granulated sugar

Preheat oven to 375 degrees.

Butter 4 12-ounce ramekins to the top. Using a rolling motion, coat ramekins with sugar. Set aside.

CRANBERRY PUREE

8 ounces dried cranberries
½ cup champagne

For the cranberry puree, combine cranberries and champagne in a food processor until smooth. Set aside.

CREME ANGLAISE

½ cup heavy cream
1½ cups half-and-half
1 cup granulated sugar, divided
6 egg yolks
1 teaspoon vanilla extract

For the crème anglaise, heat cream and half-and-half in a small pot with ½ cup sugar.

In a small heatproof bowl, combine the egg yolks and remaining sugar.

When cream mixture comes to a boil, pour it slowly over eggs and sugar, stirring constantly. Stir in the vanilla.

Pour the crème anglaise back into the pot, and heat on medium heat. Continue to cook and stir constantly, without letting it come to a boil, until thickened.

Remove from heat and strain into a bowl. Chill.

Cranberry Soufflé with Crème Anglaise

SOUFFLES

3 egg yolks
1¼ cups granulated sugar, divided
¼ cup flour
1 tablespoon cornstarch
2 cups whole milk, scalded
10 large egg whites
Powdered sugar for garnish

For the soufflés, combine egg yolks, ¾ cup sugar, flour, and cornstarch in a small mixing bowl and whisk until smooth. Slowly add hot scalded milk to mixture, whisking constantly until milk is incorporated. Transfer mixture into a non-aluminum saucepan and heat over medium heat. Stir constantly. Heat and stir until pastry cream thickens and boils. Do not scorch the bottom. When it reaches a boil, pour into a storage container or bowl to cool. Stir occasionally to prevent skin from forming on top.

Beat egg whites in the bowl of an electric mixer at high speed. While beating, add remaining sugar. Beat until soft peaks form.

With a rubber spatula, fold egg whites, 8 ounces cranberry puree, and pastry cream into a bowl. Reserve remaining cranberry puree. Stir mixture and pour into ramekins. Keep edges of ramekins clean.

Place soufflés on lowest rack of oven. Leave 6-8" space above the ramekins to allow soufflés to rise. Bake for 25-30 minutes. Tops of soufflés should be browned.

Garnish tops of soufflés with powdered sugar and remaining cranberry puree, and serve chilled crème anglaise on the side.

Tip: You can make ice cream out of the crème anglaise if you put it in an ice-cream maker.

Violet Soufflé

Violet Soufflés

These soufflés are unique because of the candied violets from Toulouse, which have an intense flavor and color.

Yields 4 individual soufflés

½ cup butter
1 cup granulated sugar, divided
1 cup candied violets, divided
3 egg yolks
¼ cup flour
1 tablespoon cornstarch
2 cups whole milk, scalded
10 large egg whites
Powdered sugar for garnish
Crème anglaise, chilled (see index)

Preheat oven to 375 degrees.

Butter 4 12-oz. ramekins to the top. Using a rolling motion, coat ramekins with ¼ cup sugar. Set aside.

Using a mortar and pestle, crush ½ cup violets to consistency of powdered sugar. Set aside.

For the soufflés, combine egg yolks, ¾ cup sugar, flour, and cornstarch in a small mixing bowl and whisk until smooth. Slowly add hot scalded milk to mixture, whisking constantly until milk is incorporated. Transfer mixture into a non-aluminum saucepan and heat over medium heat. Stir constantly. Heat and stir until pastry cream thickens and boils. Do not scorch the bottom. When it reaches a boil, pour into a storage container or bowl to cool. Stir occasionally to prevent skin from forming on top.

Beat egg whites in the bowl of an electric mixer at high speed. While beating, add the crushed violets. Beat until soft peaks form.

With a rubber spatula, fold egg whites and pastry cream into a bowl. Stir mixture and pour into ramekins. Keep edges of ramekins clean.

Place soufflés on lowest rack of oven. Leave 6-8″ space above the ramekins to allow soufflés to rise. Bake for 25-30 minutes. Tops of soufflés should be browned.

Garnish tops of soufflés with powdered sugar and remaining candied violets, and serve chilled with crème anglaise on the side.

Tip: Crush the violets with a mortar and pestle to reach the consistency of powdered sugar.

Chocolate Soufflé with Chocolate Sauce

Chocolate Soufflés with Chocolate Sauce

Here is a rise bestselling dessert!

Yields 4 individual soufflés

½ cup butter
¼ cup granulated sugar

Preheat oven to 375 degrees.

Butter 4 12-ounce ramekins to the top. Using a rolling motion, coat ramekins with sugar. Set aside.

CHOCOLATE SOUFFLES

3 egg yolks
1¼ cups granulated sugar, divided
¼ cup flour
1 tablespoon cornstarch
2 cups whole milk, scalded
1 tablespoon unsweetened cocoa powder
10 large egg whites

For the soufflés, combine egg yolks, ¾ cup sugar, flour, and cornstarch in a small mixing bowl and whisk until smooth. Slowly add hot scalded milk to mixture, whisking constantly until milk is incorporated. Transfer mixture into a non-aluminum saucepan and heat over medium heat. Stir constantly. Heat and stir until pastry cream thickens and boils. Do not scorch the bottom. When it reaches a boil, pour into a storage container or bowl to cool. Stir occasionally to prevent skin from forming on top.

Add cocoa and mix well. Set aside.

Beat egg whites in the bowl of an electric mixer at high speed. While beating, add remaining sugar. Beat until soft peaks form.

With a rubber spatula, fold egg whites and pastry cream into a bowl. Stir. Pour mixture into ramekins. Keep edges of ramekins clean.

Place soufflés on lowest rack of oven. Leave 6-8″ space above the ramekins to allow soufflés to rise. Bake for 25-30 minutes. Tops of soufflés should be browned.

CHOCOLATE SAUCE

1 cup heavy cream
1 cup half-and-half
½ cup granulated sugar
½ pound bittersweet chocolate morsels
Powdered sugar for garnish

For the chocolate sauce, while the soufflés are baking, heat a medium saucepan over medium heat. Place cream, half-and-half, granulated sugar, and chocolate in pan and mix well. Bring sauce to a boil while whipping occasionally. Remove from heat when it reaches a boil.

Dust tops of chocolate soufflés with powdered sugar. Pour chocolate sauce over soufflés.

"But, Mom! I don't want to be a chicken.
I want to be a soufflé."

Jesus Franco

5

The Childhood You Wish You Had

Children gravitate towards bright colors and want to touch, press, and hold all objects you place in front of them. It's only natural that this sensory experimentation should transition to bright and exciting foods. Children want food that tastes good and is interactive.

Hedda once met a little girl who came to visit her at her farm in Texas, and she offered the five-year-old an artichoke. The artichoke, a green thistle-like plant with sharp bracts, fascinated the little girl and later instilled in her a desire for culinary exploration. Hedda recounts that the same girl came back to the restaurant on a recent occasion and ordered the escargot soufflé. Hedda beamed with excitement as she realized that the girl had blossomed into a young lady with a very refined palate. This young lady later told Hedda that it was thanks to her that she had become so adventurous with her food choices. The artichoke had opened the little girl's eyes to a whole other culinary world, and she couldn't wait to taste the next intriguing dish set before her.

Cooking for children requires creativity. A simple meal can be just as memorable as an elaborate concoction. Letting pure and simple ingredients speak for themselves is sometimes the best manner in which to cook.

When Hedda was nine years old, her parents took her to San Miguel, Mexico. One day they decided to make their own lunch, so her father took out a little olive oil, herbs, and pasta and mixed them together, creating a simple and delicious meal.

Hedda believes that children learn by example. If parents simply pour a meal out of a package or drizzle a dressing out of a plastic bottle, the child will later follow the parents' example. Making a dressing of olive oil, lemon juice, salt, and pepper can be just as fast and easy as reaching for bottled dressing.

Parents can inspire their children to participate in preparing or enjoying a meal; all it takes is a little imagination. At rise, the meal experience becomes interactive for children. Chef Brahmi sometimes allows the children to whip the egg whites for the soufflés in a big bowl with a whisk. You can see a spark go off in their little minds; they think they are chefs as well.

Children light up when they know they can be helpful. Whether we let them be mini chefs for an afternoon or we delegate some of the responsibilities associated with preparing dinner such as setting the table, children enjoy being a part of the process. Once children finish their meal at rise, they are invited to search the restaurant for two brass frogs, Michelle and Pierre, which they may keep when they find them. The frogs are then replaced with new ones for children to seek out.

Eating should be a celebration for both adults and children. Like adults, children do not need to settle for an average meal. A celebratory meal can be as simple as combining two to three ingredients. The celebration will happen on your palate and in your spirit. The secret to creating a unique experience is in selecting seasonal ingredients.

As Hedda states, children should understand where their food comes from. They should have a proper understanding of the journey of their food. Years ago, Hedda took her son, then a little boy, to a dairy farm so that he could see that milk didn't come from a carton but from a cow. Hedda and André milked a cow, took the milk home, and made their own butter after the cream rose to the top. She made her son value the process of farm to table. A true and unique experience happens when people understand the wealth of the soil surrounding them. "People who live close to the earth have a different experience and respect for their food," says

Michelle the frog

Hedda. Teaching our children to respect what we place in front of them is essential for them to enjoy the experience of food. If we spend a little time showing our children that the earth provides us with delicious food, and encourage them to treat the earth with respect and gratitude and not overindulge in its treasures, we can nurture this beneficial symbiotic relationship.

Hedda was born in Kentucky and grew up in Tennessee. She spent summers in France with her maternal grandmother. Hedda's grandmother had a very clever way of demonstrating an important life lesson to Hedda as a child. Her grandmother told her not to throw away pieces of string or rubber bands when she came across them. That way, she would never need to purchase any. Her mother saved wrapping paper and ribbon from gifts she received to use them to wrap other gifts. Hedda's grandparents, like many of our grandparents and parents, were war survivors. Their daily vocabulary included words such as "ration," "save," and "survive." They remember that food was once hard to come by, and they developed an appreciation for it. Our past helps our children understand that food cannot be taken for granted.

Good food and good conversation dominated Hedda's childhood. Her mother gathered the family at the table for dinner every night. Eating was a communal act and a way of keeping the family together—a vehicle for sharing the laughs and worries of the day with those you love.

The family would have guests over for dinner, and many of them were fascinating characters, intrigued by Hedda's mother's culinary talents. Some guests would come over and cook as well. Hedda remembers a particular evening when one of the guests, a famous painter, Edward Giobbi, charred a pepper on the stovetop. A spark went off in Hedda's mind. It opened a new world to her, and from that day forward, she knew she was destined to be involved with food.

Shelby Foote, the noted Civil War author and a friend of the family, would also attend some of the family dinners, contributing great conversation along with his famous pot roast. Hedda quickly learned that her parents' adult friends could be interesting, as opposed to intimidating and conversationally off limits for a child.

Chef Brahmi introduced French and Algerian cooking to his children at a very young age, and his mother's couscous recipe quickly became a favorite for them. They would request the couscous all the time, asking their father to make it so they could bring it to school for the other children to taste. Cherif would occasionally take them to get fast food, and the children would get so excited about the toys. "They would throw the food away and keep the toy," he recalls proudly. Most children indulge in fast food so often that the "treat" aspect of getting a meal and a toy loses its luster. Moreover, the food is so overly processed and salty that the child becomes deficient in the nutrients he or she needs. A typical chicken nugget at these fast-food places has a staggering thirty or more ingredients, ranging from chicken meat and skin to flour, starches, and oils. The end product is more of a science experiment than a healthy meal. A healthier, economically viable, and fast option would be to pick up a whole roasted chicken, which still looks and tastes like a chicken, at your local grocery store.

Most of our culinary adventures begin at a very tender age, when everything is novel and interesting. Parents play a very prominent role in determining a child's interaction with food. "If somebody hadn't nurtured me as a child, I wouldn't be here today," explains Hedda. Enjoying food, whether we cook it or not, helps children set a positive attitude towards food and encourages them to try new food items.

Food has the ability to make you travel through time. It can conjure up childhood memories of a first time trying a wonderful food or an experience surrounding the food you enjoyed. The most poignant recollection inspired by the simple taste of a madeleine[1] can be found in Marcel Proust's *Remembrance of Things Past*.[2] The taste of a madeleine brings back to life a distant memory from his childhood, when he used to enjoy his aunt Léonie's madeleines on Sunday mornings, dipped in her cup of tea.

Hedda believes that a first time with a certain food is always magical. If you have already tasted something before, you must remember to pause and center yourself in order to recapture the magic of that first time.

Hedda's "madeleines" are grapes. Her grandmother used to peel them, and they would sit and enjoy them together. Hedda does not peel them when she eats them now. However, they always remind her of those times spent talking with her grandmother. Another food memory is the cherries she used to pick with her brother. She would eat some and wear some as cherry earrings.

There are so many firsts during childhood that if you are not of a sensitive disposition, you could easily forget them all. Hedda remembers fondly the first items she ever cooked, when she was

Kate

just seven years old, in her grandmother's kitchen. They made *biscuits grand-mère* (lemon cookies) and *gateau au chocolat*. And she will never forget her grandmother's roast chicken. Tastes from Hedda's childhood linger at the restaurant, which serves cookies similar to those she made with her grandmother, as well as artichokes Andrée, based on her mother's recipe.

Growing up, Hedda remembers that chores were always a part of family life. Her father would ask her to rake leaves or gather firewood, and the reward would always be quality time spent with family and enjoying a meal. Hedda was grateful for the chores, because they brought her closer to her family.

Cherif, one of eight children, would often go into the kitchen to see if he could help his mother. He did so not only because she truly needed a lending hand but also because he would get to spend time with her.

Some people find exaltation in front of the hanging gardens of Babylon, the pyramids of Egypt, or the statue of Zeus at Olympia, but Hedda finds beatitude in children. In her eyes, everything they say or notice is a little miracle. Our children are paving the roads of tomorrow, so why look to the past seven wonders of the world when we have children performing even greater miracles before our very eyes?

Eric's chariot des fromages

In France, there is a saying about children: *"La vérité sort de la bouche des enfants"*—the truth comes out of the mouths of children. Young children see the world without the filter that society has yet to impose on them. They view life in a different light, and this allows them to make clear and truthful observations. Hedda insists that she would rather receive criticism about her restaurant from a child, because they are so honest and insightful.

On a recent occasion, a nine-year-old girl, Kate, came to rise with her family. She immediately impressed Hedda with her sophisticated, beyond-her-years palate and her mental acuity. Hedda asked Kate if she knew what she would like to become

when she grew up. In her ear, Hedda whispered, "A chef?" Kate was surprised that Hedda had uncovered her secret aspiration.

Hedda asked Kate if she would like to fill out an application for a chef position at the restaurant one day. Kate lit up and took a pen to do so immediately. She wrote on the application that she was pursuing a position as a "cheese chef."

Hedda later called Kate's father to ask if she would like to come and apprentice a couple of hours a week at the restaurant. He agreed, as long as it would not interfere with her homework. It was arranged for Kate to come to the restaurant on weekends.

"When you see someone with raw talent like that, you have

NAME	ORIGIN	TYPE	MILK	PASTEURIZED	GIROLLE	TEXTURE	Fat %	DESCRIPTION
Bleu d'Auvergne	France	Blue	Cow	No		Crumbly	50	Vertually the same as the Fourme below.
Fourme d'Ambert	France	Blue	Cow	No		Crumbly	50	Full flavored authentic bleu.
Stilton	England	Blue	Cow	Yes		Crumbly	55	Classic English Blue
Cambozola	Germany	Part Blue/Double Cream	Cow	Yes		Soft	70	Layer of Gorgonzola inside a Camembert
Benning	Holland	Gouda	Goat	Yes		Very Firm		Very mild and firm textured.
Cotswold	England	Cheddar		Yes		Firm		Traditional double Gloucester with herbs (aka Pub Cheese)
Brie	France		Cow	Yes		Soft		Most common of all French cheeses
St. Andre'	France	Triple Cream		Yes		Soft	75	Similar to a Brie in flavor but taller
Boursin	France	Processed Spread	Cow	Yes		Soft	72	A processed French cream cheese spread with herbs and garlic
La Roule	France	Processed Spread	Cow	Yes		Very Soft		Another processed French cream cheese with a layer of herbs rolled inside
Gruyere	Swiss	Traditional Swiss	Cow	no*		Firm		Classic Swiss with nutty full flavor is usually, but not always pasteurized. The one in souffles is.
Tete de Moine	Swiss	Traditional Swiss	Cow	No	Yes	Firm	51	Girolles were designed specifically for this traditional Swiss
Manchego	Spain	Traditional Spanish	Sheep	Yes	Yes	Firm		Traditional cheese from Spain similar to the 2 Swiss cheeses above but milder
Chaumes	France		cow	yes		Soft		Very comparable to the better known Port Salut
Port Salut	France		Cow	Yes		Soft		Well known smooth flavored French cheese with a bright orange rind from annatto seeds
Pont l'Eveque	France		Cow	yes		Very Soft	45	
Purple Haze	American	Artisan	Goat	yes		Very Soft		Fennel pollen & lavender flavored from Cypress Grove in California
Bermuda Triangle	American	Artisan	Goat	Yes		Very Soft		Cypress Grove from California produces this unique goat cheese
Humboldt Fog	American	Artisan	Goat	Yes		Very Soft		Also a Cypress Grove product
Chevre	France	Traditional French	Goat	Yes		Very Soft		Assorted exterior coatings on a traditional French goat cheese
Boschetto Tartuffo	Italy		Cow/Sheep	Yes	Yes	Firm		Unusuall and expensive due to the infusion of black truffle shavings inside
Morbier	France	Artisan	Cow	yes		Firm	45	The "morning/night milk" cheese with the distinct layer of vegetable ash in the middle

to nurture it if you can," Hedda explains. "I wouldn't offer this to any nine-year-old, but this little girl was so special, I felt I had to help her on her soul path." Hedda thought that with Kate's passion for cheese, cooking, and the French language she would have her learn about the different cheeses on the cheese cart and offer them to guests. Kate's responsibilities also include hiding the frogs, Pierre and Michelle, for the children to find, polishing silverware, and wrapping cookies.

Hedda and the rise team are enthusiastic about Kate apprenticing at the restaurant. Richard, the chef de cuisine, gave Kate an altered green chef's jacket. Hedda smiles and tells Cherif, "She is going to be a cheese mogul one day, I think, or a partner in our Paris rise." Today Kate is impressing guests, even making a flawless cheese-cart presentation to the former first family. Jenna Bush noted that Kate is "a prodigy."

Talent must be cultivated at a young age. According to Paula Olszewski-Kubilius, Lisa Limburg-Weber, and Steven Pfeiffer in their book *Early Gifts: Recognizing and Nurturing Children's Talents*, highly gifted children can often lay the groundwork for their careers with behaviors they adopt in early childhood. They state, "People who become creative writers as adults often are voracious readers and writers as children. . . . Early signs of artistic talent include the ability to draw realistically at an early age and the ability to imitate the style of other artists."

Most psychologists agree that parents are critical influences in the development of a talent, insofar as they are the ones who encourage and nurture progress in their children.

As Hedda has discovered, talent in children is like a flower. The more you care for it, the more it will blossom. Encouragement and praise are fundamental to creating an environment for children to thrive in.

Young artist at work

Artichokes Andrée

This artichoke dish is a popular item on the rise menu. The vinaigrette is a recipe of Hedda's mother, Andrée.

Yields 4-6 servings

> 4-6 artichokes
> Water
> Salt to taste
> White pepper to taste
> 1 lemon, halved

Cut the stems off the artichokes and cut an inch off the tops.

In a large pot, cover artichokes with water until submerged.

Add salt and pepper.

Bring water to a boil.

Squeeze lemon juice into water and toss rinds in.

Cook covered for 40-45 minutes on medium-high heat.

> VINAIGRETTE
> 3 hard-boiled eggs
> 1 tablespoon Dijon mustard
> ¼ cup lemon juice
> ¼ cup apple cider vinegar
> Salt to taste
> Pepper to taste
> 1 cup olive oil
> ½ cup chopped parsley
> ¼ cup chopped chives

Artichokes Andrée

Chop egg whites finely. Reserve the yolks.

In a medium bowl, mix yolks with mustard.

Whisk in lemon juice, vinegar, salt, and pepper.

Slowly add the olive oil to emulsify.

Add chopped egg whites, parsley, and chives.

Artichokes are cooked when leaves come off without too much resistance. Remove from water and drain upside down. Scoop out the fuzzy choke at the center.

Pour vinaigrette into centers of artichokes.

Ham and Cheese Soufflé

Ham and Cheese Soufflés

This is the first soufflé Cherif learned to make in culinary school.

Yields 6 individual soufflés

4 ounces butter, divided
½ cup grated Parmesan, divided
½ cup white flour
2 cups whole milk
Salt to taste
White pepper to taste
¼ teaspoon nutmeg
2 cups grated Swiss cheese
12 ounces ham, ground
3 egg yolks
18 egg whites

Preheat oven to 375 degrees.

Butter 6 12-ounce ramekins to the top with 2 ounces butter. Using a rolling motion, coat ramekins with ¼ cup Parmesan. Set aside.

To make the roux, melt 2 ounces butter in a large pot over medium heat. Add flour and stir. Reduce heat to low. Cook for 2-3 minutes, stirring. Remove from heat to cool down.

To make the soufflé base, in a different saucepan, bring milk to a boil. Add salt, white pepper, and nutmeg.

Pour hot milk slowly into the roux. Bring back to a boil, stirring constantly for about 2 minutes, until the mixture thickens. Turn off the heat and keep stirring until the mixture thickens further.

Add Swiss cheese, ham, ¼ cup Parmesan, and egg yolks and stir. Make sure the mixture stays warm. This will help the soufflés rise.

In the bowl of an electric mixer, beat egg whites to soft peaks. The egg whites must have risen to peaks before you can combine with the warm mixture.

Add the warm mixture, and stir in the mixer.

Pour the mixture into ramekins, filling to the top. Keep edges of ramekins clean.

Place soufflés on lowest rack of oven. Leave 6-8″ space above the ramekins to allow soufflés to rise. Bake for 20-25 minutes. Tops of soufflés should be browned.

Tip: Use the leftover egg yolks to make crème anglaise (see index).

Spinach Soufflés

The spinach soufflé is a clever way of introducing greens into a child's diet and a satisfying way for adults to fit in their daily requirement too.

Yields 6 individual soufflés

6 ounces butter, divided
½ cup grated Parmesan, divided
½ cup white flour
2 cups whole milk
Salt to taste
White pepper to taste
½ teaspoon nutmeg, divided
½ cup grated Swiss cheese
3 egg yolks
¼ cup chopped shallots
1 tablespoon chopped garlic
1½ pounds spinach (about 6 cups)
18 egg whites

Preheat oven to 375 degrees.

Butter 6 12-ounce ramekins to the top with 2 ounces butter. Using a rolling motion, coat ramekins with ¼ cup Parmesan. Set aside.

To make the roux, melt 2 ounces butter in a large pot over medium heat. Add flour and stir. Reduce heat to low. Cook for 2-3 minutes, stirring. Remove from heat to cool down.

To make the soufflé base, in a different saucepan, bring milk to a boil. Add salt, white pepper, and ¼ teaspoon nutmeg.

Pour hot milk slowly into the roux. Bring back to a boil, stirring constantly for about 2 minutes, until the mixture thickens. Turn off the heat and keep stirring until the mixture thickens further.

Add Swiss cheese, ¼ cup Parmesan, and egg yolks and stir.

To make the spinach puree, melt 2 ounces butter over medium heat

Spinach Soufflés

in a large pot. Add shallots, garlic, salt, white pepper, and ¼ teaspoon nutmeg. Stir until shallots and garlic are translucent. Add spinach and cook until wilted, about 3-5 minutes.

Pour the mixture into a food processor, and blend until smooth.

Combine the puree and the soufflé base. Make sure the mixture stays warm. This will help the soufflés rise.

In the bowl of an electric mixer, beat egg whites to soft peaks. The egg whites must have risen to peaks before you can combine with the warm mixture.

Add the warm mixture, and stir in the mixer.

Pour the mixture into ramekins, filling to the top. Keep edges of ramekins clean.

Place soufflés on lowest rack of oven. Leave 6-8" space above the ramekins to allow soufflés to rise. Bake for 20-25 minutes. Tops of soufflés should be browned.

Gioia Family Cheese Fondue

Gioia Family Cheese Fondue

Hedda remembers that when they ate fondue, her mother would stir it in a figure eight. Her family played a fondue game: whoever dropped bread into the fondue pot had to take a sip of wine.

Yields 4-6 servings

2 baguettes, sliced
1 garlic clove, peeled and halved lengthwise
2 cups good dry white wine (not cooking wine)
2 pounds Swiss Gruyere, grated
½ cup grated Emmenthal
½ cup grated appenzeller or fontina
1 teaspoon baking soda
¼ cup Kirsch
Pepper to taste

Slice baguettes and allow to air dry.

Rub the sides and bottom of a 10-cup fondue pot with garlic.

In a separate pan, gently heat the wine. Transfer it to the fondue pot. Light the flame under the pot.

Add cheeses to the pot, a handful at a time, and combine. Stir often to avoid clumps.

Add more wine if needed, but not too much. The fondue should have the smooth consistency of a sauce.

In a small bowl, combine baking soda and Kirsch. Add to fondue pot. The fondue should now start to foam on top.

Add pepper.

Give each guest a fondue fork, for dipping baguette slices into the fondue pot. Serve with a large green salad and cornichons.[3]

Tip: Never put a fondue pot on top of an electric or gas burner, because the pot will shatter.

Sadia's Couscous

Sadia's Couscous

Sadia, Cherif's mother, made this couscous for Cherif and his siblings often. Couscous is a traditional North African dish consisting of semolina (couscous), lamb, chicken, vegetables, and raisins. It is typically cooked in a couscoussière, *a steamer for couscous.*

Yields 8-10 servings

1 cup dried chickpeas
27 cups water, divided
4 tablespoons + 1 teaspoon salt, divided
3 cups chopped yellow onion
3 cups chopped celery
6 cups diced tomatoes
3 pounds lamb shoulder, cut into pieces
1 3-pound whole chicken
2 tablespoons cumin
2 tablespoons pepper
1 cup chopped cilantro
2 pounds medium-grain couscous
1 tablespoon olive oil
8 tablespoons unsalted butter, divided
15 ounces raisins
1 pound baby carrots
1 pound haricots verts, tips removed
1 pound baby turnips
1 pound zucchini, cut into pieces
Harissa (optional)*

Soak chickpeas overnight in 1 cup water with 1 teaspoon salt.

Bring 2 cups water to a gentle boil. Cook the chickpeas for 25-30 minutes until tender. Set aside.

For the broth, pour 18 cups water into the bottom of a *couscoussière* or a large pot. Bring to a gentle boil. Add the yellow onions, celery, tomatoes, lamb, whole chicken, cumin, 3 tablespoons salt, pepper, and cilantro. Cook for about 45 minutes.

Soak the couscous grains in 6 cups warm water and 1 tablespoon salt for 3-4 minutes. Drain excess water. Coat the *couscoussière* top or a colander with olive oil. While the broth is cooking, add the couscous to the top or colander and steam over the pot of broth for 5 minutes, until the steam goes through the grains. Remove top or colander from pot. Sprinkle on salt to taste and add 4 tablespoons butter. When butter is melted, add raisins. Place the top or colander back over the pot. Steam for another 5 minutes, until the steam plumps the raisins. Remove from pot and add remaining butter to break up any clumps of grains. Set couscous aside.

Remove chicken from the pot after 45 minutes, cut into pieces, and set aside. Add carrots, *haricots verts*, turnips, zucchini, and drained chickpeas to the broth. Cook for another 10 minutes.

Serve the broth hot in a tagine[4] with chicken, couscous, and harissa on the side and hot fresh mint tea (recipe follows.)

*Harissa is a red-hot paste, which complements the couscous very nicely. It is available at specialty or international gourmet stores.

Fresh Mint Tea

Fresh Mint Tea

A custom in North African countries is to serve 3 cups of tea to guests. In the Sahara desert, the 3 cups are meant to illustrate the following: "The first cup of tea is sour as life. The second cup is sweet as love. The third is soft as death." The head of the family usually prepares the tea.

Yields 6 cups

6 cups boiling water
2 tablespoons loose green tea
1 cup fresh whole mint leaves, stems removed
Sugar to taste (optional)

Pour the boiling water into a teapot. Add green tea and mint. Allow to steep for 3-5 minutes. Add sugar if desired. Pour into traditional glasses.

Chocolat Chaud (Hot Chocolate)

Chocolat Chaud (Hot Chocolate)

This is Hedda's favorite recipe for chocolat chaud, *which she enjoys every morning at rise.*

Yields 1 serving

8 ounces whole milk
2 tablespoons semisweet chocolate morsels
Sugar to taste
Whipped cream (optional)

In a medium saucepan, bring the milk to a boil.

Stir in the chocolate morsels until well incorporated.

Add sugar.

Serve hot, with whipped cream if desired.

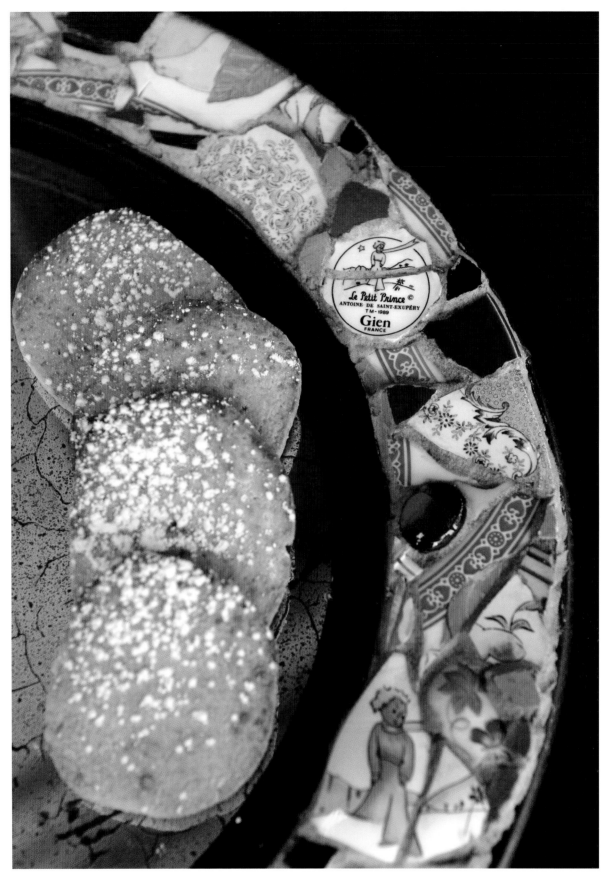

Biscuits Grand-mère

Biscuits Grand-mère

These cookies are from Hedda's grandmother's kitchen, where Hedda learned to make and love them. Cherif adapted the recipe for the restaurant.

Yields 20-22 cookies

> Zest of 3 lemons
> 1 cup butter
> 3½ cups all-purpose flour
> ¾ cup sugar
> 3 eggs, divided
> 1 tablespoon milk
> Powdered sugar (optional)

Preheat oven to 350 degrees.

Combine the lemon zest, butter, flour, and sugar in a food processor and blend.

Add 2 eggs and mix well. Form dough by hand.

Roll into cylinder that is 2½" wide. Wrap in plastic wrap to form a more uniform cylinder, and remove wrap. Cut dough into ½" slices. Arrange on a baking sheet.

Combine 1 egg with milk to make an egg wash. Brush on top of slices.

Bake for 15-20 minutes until golden brown.

Dust with powdered sugar, if desired.

Andrée's Orange Surprise

Andrée's Orange Surprise

Hedda grew up eating these frozen orange treats, which her mother prepared for the family. The highlight of this treat was to find the hidden chocolate in one of the oranges.

Yields 6-8 servings

> 6-8 medium oranges
> 1 small piece chocolate
> 1 cup heavy whipping cream
> 2 tablespoons Grand Marnier
> 1 can (8 ounces) frozen orange juice, room
>   temperature
> 1 quart orange sherbet

Slice the tops off the oranges, and shave a thin slice off the bottoms so they may sit upright. Reserve the sliced tops and shaved bottoms.

Juice oranges without breaking the skin, and hollow them with a spoon. Set juice aside and discard pulp. Place the shaved bottoms inside oranges to reinforce the inside and prevent leaks.

Place chocolate inside one of the oranges, which will be the surprise part of the dish.

Freeze hollow oranges for 1 hour or until rock hard.

Place cream and Grand Marnier in the bowl of an electric mixer fitted with the whisk attachment. Beat on high speed until just before peaks start to form. Add fresh and canned orange juice and sherbet, and blend.

Remove oranges from the freezer, and pour the mixture into each orange, filling to the top. Fit the reserved lid on top of each orange.

Freeze for 2 hours. Remove 20 minutes before serving.

Tip: To keep the oranges upright in the freezer, roll medium-sized pieces of aluminum foil into 6-8 individual collars and place 1 around the bottom of each orange.

Cherry Clafouti

Cherry Clafouti

Clafouti is a traditional French dessert originating from the Limousin region. The most typical French clafoutis are made with cherries, but cherries are not always in season and readily available. You can substitute blueberries, pears, apples, plums, or peaches for the cherries.

Yields 8-10 servings

1 tablespoon butter
½ cup sugar
¾ cup flour
1 cup heavy whipping cream
½ tablespoon vanilla
3 eggs
1 pound cherries, pitted
Powdered sugar (optional)

Preheat oven to 375 degrees.

Butter an ovenproof 10″ round dish.

In a mixing bowl, whisk together the sugar, flour, cream, vanilla, and eggs.

Arrange cherries in ovenproof dish.

Pour the batter over the cherries.

Bake for 15-20 minutes, until browned on top.

Dust the *clafouti* with powdered sugar, if desired.

Serve the *clafouti* warm or at room temperature.

Cheese poubelle

6

Green Living

Just like charity, being green begins at home. If you cook with a green approach, you will make great food while being mindful of your environment.

Rise grows its own herbs in the planters on the terrace and in the front garden, in addition to ordering some. Herbs are easy to maintain and are a fundamental part of the dishes at the restaurant.

Rise has also devised a way to creatively repurpose remnants from their cheese cart, with their house recipe, the cheese *poubelle.* Cherif blends the different cheeses with herbs, dried fruit, and spirits, and the result is simply delicious.

The vinegar is made in-house, in French wine barrels, using white and red wine. Rise sells the barrels to guests. The restaurant takes on the appeal of a Cordon Bleu cooking institution, with its staff teaching you how to make your own vinegar.

The *salon de soufflé* encourages patrons to make their own versions of what they enjoy at the restaurant. A favorite is the seltzer water, for which guests can purchase the seltzer bottle and cartridges at rise. The cartridges come from wells with natural minerals in Austria and Hungary. Guests can recreate their own seltzer within half an hour.

Hedda remembers that her grandmother always kept the root of an onion and the feet of a chicken, rather than discarding them. She would later use those items to create a flavorful stock.

Having spent every summer in France as a child, Hedda developed a fondness for markets. She enjoyed the ritual of going with her grandfather and watching him carefully select produce and speak with the different vendors and people of the town. When Hedda travels abroad today, she prefers to rent a house with a kitchen, so that she can go to the local market and cook

at home. She feels an intimate connection with the purveyors, an esprit de corps, which she would not experience if she were eating at a restaurant. What she most admires about the vendors at French markets is the pride they have for the produce they sell. On one visit, a purveyor was selling figs stuffed with foie gras, which Hedda could not purchase since she was flying back to the United States. The lady at the stand offered her a taste instead, so Hedda could experience the decadence of this surprising combination.

In some of these small towns, the residents have small refrigerators that can hold only one or two days' worth of food. Their food does not go bad because it is soon eaten. People buy just what they need and nothing more.

Cherif does the same when he cooks at home. He goes to the grocery store or the farmer's market the same day he decides to cook. This allows him to use everything he buys, without wasting produce or forgetting about it in the refrigerator. It also means that his ingredients are always fresh.

Eating locally is a means to being green. When you purchase produce that is grown in your area, the farmers do not need to ship it across the country or globe. The second important factor to eating locally is eating seasonally. This allows you to pay a little less than you would pay for the same product if it came from Chile or China.

However, eating locally isn't always for everyone. Cherif explains that mozzarella from Italy, for instance, is very different from the kind we can buy in the United States. Some ingredients just taste better from certain regions.

Hedda's raison d'être[1] is to be around food. She can eat it, cook it, or simply exist in a food environment. "Some women

spend $800 on shoes. I could spend that on food. Think of how many people I could have over!" she says excitedly. Hedda has a green approach to clothing as well. She wears her mother and her grandmother's clothes, the warmth of her loved ones enveloping and comforting her. She feels connected to her family through the threads of their clothes, her cherished heirlooms. There is a melancholic beauty that is associated with clothing from our parents' and grandparents' eras. The fabrics feel rich and sturdy enough to outlast time itself.

7

The Art of Setting the Table

The first thing Hedda will tell you about setting the perfect table is that there is no such thing as a "perfect" table. She firmly believes that a home cook can create a wonderful atmosphere whether the linens are matching or not. A table needs to be inviting, not intimidating, and it must be a reflection of the meal you prepare and the company you keep.

Hedda's mother, who was also her mentor, was a perfectionist. With no professional training, she was a gifted cook who served delectable food from her modest kitchen. While living in Tennessee, Hedda's mother was able to make dishes with ingredients that seemed as though they could have come from Oregon, California, or France. She would create the entire meal, try it first, and then serve it to her family or guests. She would also isolate herself in the kitchen and not partake in any conversation, so as not to make errors. She was not a good teacher, because she wanted no interruptions or questions while she was preparing a meal.

Unlike her mother, Hedda believes in cooking with people around her. And if she happens to mess up because she was too immersed in conversation, she just laughs about it. She remembers her mother's ideas about setting the table: "She ironed a tablecloth. I take it out of the dryer and stick it on the table."

Hedda also recalls her mother's attention to detail and tradition for the family's Easter dinners. She would use eighteenth-century pewter flower molds to make ice cream. The table was always artistic and uniquely hers.

As a child, Hedda was impressed by fingerbowls at her aunt's house. They had beautiful violets floating in them. She liked that a flower from the garden became part of their meal. Hedda believes in picking flowers from her garden or putting herbs in her arrangements. She enjoys repeating an element from the meal on the table. Oftentimes, when you buy fresh parsley, you only use a small portion of it to cook and are left with a large bunch, big enough for a small flower arrangement.

In restaurants, serving hot food to guests can be a challenge. Cherif believes that the soufflé is the ideal dish to serve, because you waste no time or heat transferring it onto another dish. It goes into the oven in its little ramekin and arrives on the guest's table in that same ramekin. When Cherif entertains, he expects his guests to be ready to eat. He loves when guests just begin eating as soon as he places the dish on the table.

When Hedda is alone, she will cook an extraordinary meal just for herself, with an appealing presentation. She finds pleasure in a good dish or in watching and listening to the bubbles rush up from the bottom of a champagne flute. People often cook to impress their guests, forgetting that a meal can be as rewarding as watching a sunrise. A meal can be beautiful scenery waiting to be taken in.

André, Hedda's son, remembers what his mother prized at the table: "It was a feast every time. Nothing was rushed."

Setting the table is a way to demonstrate to your guests who you are. It is an opportunity to unleash your creativity. Having lived full time on a remote Texas farm, Hedda knows that being resourceful is essential if you want to put together an inviting table. She will throw a vintage blanket on a table as a tablecloth and transform a shotgun cartridge into a candleholder, an artichoke into a flower, and a pool-ball rack into a great fresh farm egg display, with an eight ball in the middle. A Maasai spear, gun, and duck press quickly become the centerpieces of her hunter's table.

Large wooden crayons, Scrabble letters spelling out little guests' names, and antique toys transform a large, green, concrete coffee table into a children's table.

Creating an inviting table setting becomes somewhat of a treasure hunt, where one searches one's home for something intriguing to use on the table. Those pieces and heirlooms are also great conversation starters. Hedda tells us her Maasai spear is from one of the trips her parents took to Africa in the 1960s.

In typical Texas fashion, once the meal reaches an end, Hedda's guests often get to shoot clay pigeons with a shotgun like the one found on the table. There are no defined boundaries between the inside and outside of her house. Just like a Frank Lloyd Wright home, the architecture is organic, and it becomes part of the meal.

Oysters with Mignonette Sauce

Oysters with Mignonette Sauce

For Christmas and New Year's Eve dinner, the French turn to these delicacies to celebrate. Oysters make a festive appetizer all year round.

Yields 2 servings

12 oysters, cleaned and shucked
4 tablespoons chopped shallots
4 tablespoons red wine vinegar
4 tablespoons white wine
Salt to taste
Pepper to taste

Arrange the oysters on a dish, on the half-shell.

Mix shallots, vinegar, wine, salt, and pepper to make the mignonette sauce.

Pour mignonette over oysters.

Serve chilled.

Escargots in Shells

Escargots in Shells

This classic escargot preparation with parsley butter will leave your guests in awe.

Yields 8-10 servings

1 can extra-large snails
1 cup (8 ounces) butter, divided
1 cup + 2 tablespoons chopped shallots, divided
½ cup + 1 tablespoon chopped garlic, divided
4-5 sprigs thyme
2 small bay leaves
Salt to taste
Pepper to taste
½ cup chopped parsley, chopped

Preheat oven to 375 degrees.

Rinse and drain snails.

In a large pot, heat ½ cup butter over medium heat. Add 1 cup shallots, ½ cup garlic, the thyme, and bay leaves and cook until translucent.

Add snails. Cook 5 minutes. Season with salt and pepper.

For the parsley butter, place the parsley, 2 tablespoons shallots, 1 tablespoon garlic, salt, and pepper in a mortar. Add 1 small piece butter at a time from the remaining ½ cup butter, and blend with pestle.

Place 1-2 prepared escargots in each shell and top each with 1 tablespoon parsley butter.

Bake escargots in shells for 10-15 minutes until butter sizzles.

Tip: The parsley butter is ideal for spreading on toast, tossing in a pasta dish, or topping grilled or baked fish.

Lobsters Celine

Lobsters Celine

This classic French lobster dish features Celine brandy sauce.

Yields 4-6 servings

2 egg yolks
½ tablespoon Dijon mustard
Salt to taste
Pepper to taste
2 tablespoons cider vinegar
Juice of 1 lemon
1 tablespoon brandy
⅓ cup ketchup
2 cups canola oil
2 (2-pound) lobsters, cleaned, halved, and cooked

For the Celine brandy sauce, in the bowl of an electric mixer, blend the yolks and mustard. Season with salt and pepper.

Add vinegar, lemon juice, brandy, and ketchup.

Slowly add canola oil until all ingredients are incorporated.

Serve the lobsters chilled, with the Celine brandy sauce on the side.

Tip: For a different presentation, line martini glasses with endives. Remove the lobster meat from the shells, and arrange over endives with sliced avocado and Celine brandy sauce.

The Painter Pasta

The Painter Pasta

When Cherif first witnessed artist and cookbook author Ed Giobbi making a dried pasta dish, he was in awe. This recipe is Cherif's interpretation of Ed's pasta. Mr. Giobbi, like Hedda and Cherif, always looks forward to sitting at the table and eating with friends and family. He feels that, at his parents' house, "the table was like a prayer bench."

Yields 6-8 servings

16-20 shrimp, peeled and deveined
4 tablespoons olive oil
2 tablespoons minced garlic
2 teaspoons crushed red peppers
¼ cup minced basil
½ pound dried penne pasta, uncooked
1 pound tomatoes, diced
Salt to taste
Pepper to taste
2½ cups water
16-20 clams in closed shells
1 head broccoli, cut into florets
¼ cup shaved imported Parmesan

Rinse shrimp under running water.

In a skillet or large pan, heat the olive oil over medium heat.

Add garlic, crushed red peppers, and basil and stir for 2 minutes.

Add the pasta, and stir to coat with olive oil.

Add the tomatoes, salt, and pepper and stir.

Turn the heat to high and add the water. Bring to a boil. Reduce heat and simmer for 5 minutes.

Stir in the clams, and cook for 3-4 minutes until they open.

Add the broccoli and shrimp. Stir. Cook for another 3-4 minutes.

Sprinkle Parmesan on top. Serve hot.

Niçoise Salad

Niçoise Salad

This salad composed of tuna, potatoes, green beans, black olives, capers, and egg originates from Nice, France. Most **salade niçoise** *purists insist on anchovies and canned tuna, but we prefer this simple and tasty interpretation with seared tuna. Niçoise olives are very small. Use the black variety for this recipe.*

Yields 1-2 servings

6 ounces tuna (sashimi grade)
¼ cup black and white sesame seeds
Salt to taste
Pepper to taste
1 tablespoon olive oil
3 cups mesclun salad greens, washed and dried
4 ounces green beans, cooked
4 ounces fingerling potatoes, roasted and cut in
   chunks
¼ cup niçoise olives, pitted
1 tablespoon minced red onion
½ tablespoon capers, drained
Cherry tomatoes, halved
1 hard-boiled egg, sliced

Coat tuna with sesame seeds. Season with salt and pepper. In a skillet with the olive oil, sear it rare for 1-2 minutes. Slice.

Arrange mesclun, green beans, potatoes, olives, onion, capers, tomatoes, and egg on a plate. Place tuna on top.

Yields 10 servings

VINAIGRETTE

3 tablespoons Dijon mustard
¼ cup apple cider vinegar
Salt to taste
Pepper to taste
1 ½ cups olive oil

For the vinaigrette, in a bowl, whisk the mustard, vinegar, salt, and pepper. Slowly add the olive oil to emulsify.

Drizzle 1-2 tablespoons atop salad.

Apricot Galette

Apricot Galette

This warm and comforting dessert hails from Hedda's mother's kitchen.

Yields 1 12" galette

2½ cups all-purpose flour
4 tablespoons fine sugar, divided
½ teaspoon kosher salt
1 cup (8 ounces) unsalted butter, cut into ½"
   pieces and chilled
⅔ cup ice water
8 apricots, pitted and halved
1 cup blackberries
1 egg
1 tablespoon milk
Whipped cream (optional)

Preheat oven to 350 degrees.

In a large bowl, mix flour, 2 tablespoons sugar, and salt. Place in a blender or food processor. Add the pieces of chilled butter little by little, processing until all is evenly distributed.

Add the ice water to the flour mixture, processing until the dough begins to form a ball. You will see butter streaks.

Remove dough and form into a disk. Wrap the disk in wax paper or plastic wrap and store in the refrigerator for at least 1 hour.

On a lightly floured surface, roll out the dough until ¼" thick. Cut a 12" round, and place on a lined baking sheet. Place 1 apricot half, cut side down, on the center of the dough. Surround with some berries. Cover the rest of the tart with apricots (cut side down) and berries. Take the dough edges and fold towards the center. Sprinkle 2 tablespoons sugar all over the fruit.

In a small bowl, whisk the egg with milk to make an egg wash. Brush the crust with the egg wash.

Place on the middle rack of oven. Bake for 15-20 minutes or until golden brown. Serve with whipped cream, if desired.

Germaine's Apple Tart

Germaine's Apple Tart

Yields 1 9-10" tart

> Zest of 3 lemons
> 1¼ cups butter, divided
> 3¾ cups all-purpose flour, divided
> 1¾ cups sugar, divided
> 5 eggs, divided
> 1 tablespoon cornstarch
> 2 cups whole milk, scalded
> 6 apples, peeled, cored, halved, and thinly sliced

Preheat oven to 350 degrees.

Butter a 9-10" pie dish with ¼ cup butter.

For the dough, place the lemon zest, 1 cup butter, 3½ cups flour, and ¾ cup sugar in a food processor and blend. Add 2 eggs and mix well. Form dough by hand.

Roll out the dough with a rolling pin, and place the dough on top of the pie dish. Pat dough down into dish. Cut off excess edges.

For the pastry cream, combine 3 egg yolks, ¾ cup sugar, ¼ cup flour, and cornstarch in a small mixing bowl and whisk until smooth. Slowly add hot scalded milk to mixture, whisking constantly until milk is incorporated. Transfer mixture to a non-aluminum saucepan, and heat over medium heat. Heat and stir until pastry cream thickens and boils. Do not scorch the bottom. When it reaches a boil, pour into a storage container or bowl to cool. Stir occasionally to prevent skin from forming on top.

Place the pastry cream on top of the prepared dough.

Arrange apples vertically against each other, starting from the outside and working towards the center of the pie. Cover the whole tart with apples. Sprinkle with 2 tablespoons sugar.

Bake for 15-20 minutes until golden brown. Set aside to cool.

Dominique's Berry Tarts

Dominique's Berry Tarts

Berry tarts are seasonal desserts and are sure to please any guest from age 2 to 102.

Yields 4-6 tarts

5 eggs, divided
1½ cups sugar, divided
3¾ cups all-purpose flour, divided
1 tablespoon cornstarch
2 cups whole milk, scalded
Zest of 3 lemons
1¼ cups butter, divided
2-3 cups seasonal berries
Strawberry jam, heated and diluted

Preheat oven to 350 degrees.

For the pastry cream, combine 3 egg yolks, ¾ cup sugar, ¼ cup flour, and cornstarch in a small mixing bowl and whisk until smooth. Slowly add hot scalded milk to egg mixture, whisking constantly until milk is incorporated. Transfer mixture to a non-aluminum saucepan, and heat over medium heat. Stir constantly. Heat and stir until pastry cream thickens and boils. Do not scorch the bottom. When it reaches a boil, pour into a storage container or bowl to cool. Refrigerate. Stir occasionally to prevent skin from forming on top.

Butter 4-6 small tart dishes with ¼ cup butter.

For the dough, place lemon zest, 1 cup butter, ¾ cup sugar, and 3½ cups flour in a food processor and blend. Add 2 eggs and mix well. Form dough by hand and roll it out with a rolling pin.

Place dough on top of each tart dish. Poke all over with a fork.

Bake for 15-20 minutes until golden brown. Set aside to cool.

Fill each tart with pastry cream, and top with berries. Brush with strawberry jam to glaze the berries.

Tip: Freeze leftover dough to make *biscuits grand-mère.*

8

Life on the Farm

Singletree, Hedda's farm in Hunt County, is a haven of peace and quiet, a home away from bustling city life, and a place to take everything in.

Residential designer Frank Clements happened to be at the right place at the right time when he met Hedda and Jack. Hedda and Jack were driving down dirt roads in the country looking at different houses to get an idea for what they wanted to build on their land. They met Frank on one of those roads, where he was building a house with his father-in-law.

Inspired to build by his father, who was a carpenter, Frank had studied architecture. This launched his passion to create objects of all kinds, as unusual as wooden fountain pens, as elaborate as custom burled armoires, and as spiritual as a lighted, glass-enclosed, cherry-wood-housing shrine cabinet, measuring fifteen feet tall and forty-two feet long with three sections, for statues of Buddhist divinities for a new temple in Arlington, Texas. Frank explains, "We are still figuring out how we will get the thousand-pound Buddha in there. We are not allowed to touch him. Only the monks can touch him. I guess they will have to recruit many monks."

In November of 1980, they began construction on the farmhouse. The main house was originally planned to sit at the forefront of the property, which didn't allow for much privacy. Frank suggested building the house by the creek, with the nearby 300-year-old oak tree providing a visual frame. It took eight years to get the house close to the vision the designer and the owners had for it.

Hedda insisted she wanted the house to feel old and "lived in." She and Jack bought twelve-by-sixteen-inch wood beams from an old Canada Dry bottling plant that was about to be torn down. A majority of the framing lumber came from the floor framing of the six-story Colbert-Volk Building on Elm Street in downtown Dallas. It came with many nails, at an affordable price, and was used to build the basement, one of the upstairs bedrooms, and the deck.

Frank designed the windows to maximize the flow of air in the house and to be energy efficient. The bricks in the chimney, on the front porch, and in the living room came from a salvage company and were originally pavers in the town square of Commerce, Texas.

Jack had heard that the Adolphus hotel in Dallas was planning on having a sale to make room for new furniture as part of their renovation. Hedda and Jack found big doors from the original mezzanine meeting rooms and incorporated them in the design of the Singletree farmhouse. They repurposed the green marble reception desk as a bar in the living room. They bought a couple of commercial fridges, which turned out to be very noisy and required a little extra maintenance and attention, but they are still working and keeping food cool today. The stainless steel sinks and elaborate hardware and solid wood doors were also purchased from the hotel.

The kitchen was designed for a left-handed person. All three carpenters who built the house and Hedda are left-handed. Hedda was adamant about not wanting Formica or wooden countertops. She had mentioned to Frank that her father had poured cement on his countertops, which she found very useful since it was durable, heat resistant, and aged well. They recreated a similar countertop from cement for Hedda's kitchen. For the kitchen cabinets, Frank and Hedda used reclaimed barn wood, which Frank personally collected from nearby farms. Hedda had the idea of creating small holes in the cabinets, where she could insert her finger to pull the cabinets open rather than using the standard hardware pulls.

A view of the farm from the front of the house

The barstools in the living room came from a ballet school in London. Frank designed two main furniture pieces for the living and dining rooms. One is a heavy wooden cover to conceal the pool table. The other is a lazy Susan dining table with a battery-operated tray, which he built using an old bicycle chain and a small motor.

All of Frank's creations and construction in Hedda's farmhouse are intact today. As Frank admits, "I can probably build whatever it is you might think of." Hedda confirms that Frank, as well as being able to build just about anything, is a superb problem solver. He is proudest of his solution to keep the pool temperature comfortable during the hot summer months. The answer consists of a one-half horsepower pump that circulates heat from the pool to the two-acre farm pond near the house.

This house is a paradigm for architecture enthusiasts and proof that a dream project that is well thought through with solid foundations can become a reality. Its clean long lines, open spaces, low flat style, repetitive details, stucco, and high windows echo the style of Frank Lloyd Wright. Coincidentally, Frank's wife was Wright's great-niece. Although Wright passed away before Frank Clements met his wife, he was able to meet Wright's wife and children and spend some time in the famed house of Taliesin.

The Singletree farmhouse feels as though it has stood the test of time on this parcel of land in Texas, amid the cows, goats, and other roaming animals. Frank teased the gentleman who delivered the pool table that they were just doing a slight remodel; the house was really seventy years old, he insisted. The gullible person believed him, but once Frank told him he was joking, that was the last time he believed anything Frank said.

Frank has been an essential part of the design of rise also. He was commissioned to create a large sink in the common bathroom

area, which he custom designed and built with the help of another architect. They added some personal touches such as children's handprints and leaf prints. Frank also created the countertops in the bar area out of recycled materials.

Hedda hired two architects to design rise, and she took them back to a design aesthetic that was a departure from the commercial projects they were used to working on. When meeting with the contractors, Hedda felt as though they couldn't relate to what she wanted to create. She convinced the contractors to drive an hour to her farm to show them exactly the design style she was looking for.

When they met with Hedda again, they told her they were happy they made the trip to her farmhouse. Their initial drawings were for a very contemporary-looking restaurant, so now they would regroup.

When you stand at the door at rise, looking into the restaurant, you feel the same experience rushing through you as you do walking through the doors of Singletree farm. You feel as though you are a part of a unique experience.

Frank is an eternal student, constantly learning from his projects. And he appreciates what people are willing to divulge when they work with him.

Hedda is joined in the dining room by her dog, Lucky, and a friend

Hedda's caretaker at the farm, Ramon, is a "soulful person," Hedda explains. "We couldn't keep this place without him. He is thoughtful about everything. He cares for everything at the farm like they are his own things."

Ramon's responsibilities at Singletree farm include caring for animals, of which there are many: twenty-eight cows, nine goats, seven sheep, fifty chickens, and nine ducks. He has devised clever ways to solve problems. The mother hens, for example, like to be higher up than the little chicks in the chicken coop. So Ramon has placed Ping-Pong balls on the upper parts of the coop to keep the mothers on the ground, closer to their chicks.

When Ramon first came to work on the farm, he noticed there were no eggs. After careful observation, he realized that a nest of snakes was living under the coop and eating all the eggs. He got rid of the snakes, and when eggs go missing, he now knows why.

Ramon also has a hatching system, which consists of numbering eggs for the three-week hatch duration, in the event that hens lay eggs next to each other at different times. If the hen leaves early, the eggs won't hatch. With this system, Ramon is able to make sure the eggs are being hatched after the full three weeks.

Another animal needing special attention is the property's large bull. He tends to pick fights with neighboring bulls, so Ramon had to build a big wire enclosure for him. Ramon also must keep the calves separate from their mothers periodically, because they tend to drink more milk than they need to.

The goats have come to see Ramon as more than just a caretaker; two little goats view him as their enabler. Ramon steps into their enclosure and holds their mother still so they can get some milk

Ramon Sanchez

from her. He has also taken to bottle-feeding some of the newborn animals on the farm, typically lambs and calves, when first-time mothers are unsure of what to do with their young.

Ramon's other duties on the farm include mowing the fields, fixing broken items, maintaining the tractors and other equipment, plumbing, and welding. He was never taught how to perform farming duties, but he was able to pick them up pretty quickly when he got his first job on a farm in 1997.

André, Hedda's son, enjoyed spending time with Ramon on the farm growing up, and still today when he visits, he finds time to catch up with him. André enjoyed learning from Ramon. He remembers some of the useful tricks Ramon taught him about building fences and feeding and training animals when he was a boy. These experiences allowed him to develop a strong sense of self and become independent. André remembers, "It was interesting because I learned about responsibilities and I got to see the reward in hard work."

Ramon also cares for another family's farm in Lone Oak. They built a home there for him, his wife, and their three children. Ramon prefers life on the farm to life in the city. His favorite activity is to ride on the tractor, where he can think and admire nature's treasures stretching out before him.

La fête commence!

9

Chefs Entertaining Chefs

Many chefs gathered at Hedda's farmhouse to celebrate the seventieth birthday of a man who is revered in kitchens across France and America. Jean Lafont has been a friend and mentor to all those present at his party.

In 1980, Hedda had hosted several chefs for Jean's fortieth birthday. Her farmhouse was not quite ready for entertaining, however. It was still under construction; the restrooms were not yet finished and the counters were framed but had no tops. The chefs made do, bringing a refrigerated truck loaded with enough food for Hedda's entire county. Each chef was responsible for bringing or preparing one dish, and Cherif made the birthday cake. Jean Banchet, a renowned French chef and owner of Le Français in Wheeling, Illinois, attended. He trained under French master Fernand Point, who is considered one of the finest chefs of the twentieth century.

One of the chefs, Mohammed, had no sooner reached the property when he saw horses, ran into the field, and jumped on one. It was a real party, and a memorable birthday for Jean, which inspired Hedda and Cherif to recreate a similar event for Jean's seventieth birthday.

When you look at these men, with their proud demeanors and smiles across their faces, you share in their excitement of belonging to something akin to a fraternity of the pan and whisk—a fraternity where the "hazing" consists of the grueling dinner service of great restaurants, with hungry customers clamoring for your food. And together, they fight through the dinner service, bonding over the lit stoves.

Richard Bertschi, a chef manager at rise, explains that in a kitchen environment, you learn very quickly to work together. He remembers when he first worked with Cherif in Dallas at the Oz Club, a restaurant in the seventies. Cherif was not yet as fluent as he wanted to be. Swiss-American Richard acted as his translator, while Cherif taught him some classical cooking techniques.

Jean Lafont runs a kitchen like a business. But the minute the stove is turned off, and he is done shouting orders over the brouhaha of the sizzling and chopping, he invites everyone out for drinks. "Outside I was a different man, but inside I was tough," admits Jean.

Jean taught many chefs who are now culinary masters around the world. Some are in Singapore, Jamaica, France, and Japan, but the distance doesn't stop them from keeping in touch with the man who taught them how to cook. Jean told them, "When I pray at night, I say thank you for having worked with all these guys that are here today." Jean did what other chefs did for him. He taught as well as he could, and if that meant being tough, then so be it.

"He has very high standards, and a lot of people don't live up to them. It's not easy," Richard observes. Richard remembers his first few days working under Jean. "One night, I was so disappointed in myself for not doing better that I left in tears. But I came back." Richard knew that if he wanted to improve his culinary talents, he would have to persevere and learn through his mistakes. "It was quite an education," says Richard.

Richard's fondest memory from working with Jean was his constantly reiterating: "You are soft like liver. I am going to make you like steel." Jean wanted to make his chefs as resilient as possible, like a good Roman legion officer.

Richard shares that his path is different from the one he originally set out on. "I went to Texas A&M to be a chemical engineer, and now I work with fresh food." Although he had different dreams for himself, he is thankful every day for the

Cherif Brahmi, Richard Bertschi, and Antonio Avona

path that he chose and the people he met along the way. Richard cherishes the lessons he learned over the years in his father's kitchen and all the kitchens he has worked in. "If you want to be in charge of the kitchen, you have to be in charge of yourself."

Jean's wife was always the decision maker of the household, determining where the family would move and which restaurant offers Jean should take. This led him to Baltimore, where he was treated like a king, he says. Phil Vaccaro, who ran a stable of prestigious restaurants in Dallas, asked to speak to Jean's wife one day, and this led the Lafont family to relocate to Dallas and run Vaccaro Restaurants.

Jean Lafont started working in kitchens at a very young age. He apprenticed under some of the best chefs in France, eventually moving up the culinary ladder to became a notable chef himself. He worked at the Plaza Athenée in Paris for many years and the Savoy Hotel in London. He moved to New York, where he worked at the Rainbow Room. There he ran 1,000-cover evenings, a major departure from the smaller settings of the Plaza and Savoy.

Jean's kitchens were primarily run by a group of Frenchmen. One daring American wanted to break this tradition: Jim Deibel. One evening, Jim's friend suggested they borrow his father's membership card to the Oz Club and bring dates for dinner. The

Oz Club was two weeks old, with three stories, big staircases, and a disco. Jim recognized the former bar manager from Hungry Hunter. Jim went up to him and exclaimed, "This is the neatest place I have ever seen! I want to go to work here."

The bar manager met Jim's enthusiasm with a sharp: "You have no chance. There are twenty Frenchmen and three Mexicans in the kitchen. No way you will get a job here."

Jim asked the bar manager if he could still point out the chef when he came out of the kitchen. When Lafont emerged with a big cigar in his mouth, Jim went up to him and patted him on the shoulder. "Hi, I'm Jim Deibel and I want to work for you." And Lafont cried out, "Ha!"

Jim nonetheless left his phone number on the back of a napkin. Three weeks later, he received a phone call from Jean. "The reason I gave him the job was because he was determined," he recalls. "I thought: I will give him a chance." And that is how Jim Deibel became the first American in Jean's French kitchen.

All talented chefs find their inspiration in the culinary encyclopedia, the *Larousse Gastronomique*, and their cooking skills in French classical training. "Everything has changed," Jean declares. "We used to make beautiful classical things. Now you go to school for a couple of years and you call yourself a chef." Jean Lafont trained eight years as an apprentice before he could become a chef. He laments that, due to lack of training, chefs today don't

For yesterday is but a dream,
And tomorrow is only a vision.
But today, well lived,
Makes every yesterday a dream
of happiness
And every tomorrow a vision
of hope.

Look well, therefore, to this day.

Sanskrit Proverb

Jean Lafont (with cigar) with fellow pétanque players

know how to debone something properly. He remembers fondly the times when *grande cuisine* was appreciated; he longs for the days when they would spend hours making beautiful creations out of lobster carcasses. "We would make horses, hats, and even D'Artagnans out of those lobster carcasses. Beautiful things we would make," he says pensively.

At Jean's seventieth birthday party, a giant leg of lamb and chickens roasted over a big barbecue. Louis, one of Dallas's most acclaimed pastry chefs, made a beautiful almandine cake with a funny freehanded picture of Jean chasing a younger woman with an envelope made out of marzipan and chocolate. "You see, he is pushing the envelope!" Louis comments with a chuckle.

Baking is a precise science. Cooking, on the other hand, is a more approximate art for these culinary masters. Training and experience, rather than measuring tools, dictate their knowledge of how much of an ingredient to use.

When chefs eat, they crave the very best. Louis recalls a time when he and Jean were in France, and they drove 400 miles to Genoa, Italy, to eat some pasta. They drove back after their meal. Jean admits, "*Voilà!* That's me."

Once on a drive from Atlanta to Dallas, they bought some brie and a very nice bottle of Châteauneuf-du-Pape red wine, which they savored on the road. Jean asked to take the wheel, and Louis somehow felt confident that Jean would do fine driving. But Louis woke up startled to find they were in a ditch. "We had a good time," concludes Jean.

Jean and Louis also took a trip to Saint–Tropez, where they regaled their palates with some of the best foie gras they had ever come across. The man who owned the restaurant prepared it himself. Antonio Avona, the Italian chef, trained under Jean and is a dear friend of Cherif. He reminisces about a visit to a racetrack, eating filet mignon and drinking wine with Italian and French colleagues, while the rest of the attendees were eating fried foods and drinking beer.

Cooking and eating are an essential part of a chef's life. Enjoying all foods is a part of their identities, their reason for being. Every meal needs to be as succulent and as memorable as the one before. Chefs eat as if every meal could be their last. When chefs get together, they cook. It is second nature to these men and women. Cooking is not just their day job—it consumes their entire lives. They derive immense pleasure from concocting new dishes and enjoying them together. Antonio elaborates, "Jean would come in and say, 'Let's make this new dessert.' He would make three different desserts that we taught the pastry chef and made at the restaurant."

All these foreign chefs bonded in Dallas while working together at various restaurants, and their relationships evolved from friendship to a close-knit family. "It has been a very close family," Antonio adds. "There is a lot of love. I always said that Dallas is such a melting pot that your friends become your family."

In France, there is an expression that was made famous by the 1959 François Truffaut film *Les Quatre Cents Coups* (*The 400 Blows*). The film's title means "to raise hell." From the sound of their stories, the French and Italian chefs present at this birthday party have definitely done the *quatre cents coups* together. When at work, they work, and when they are off the clock, there is no telling what tricks they are up to.

Yet the beauty of their craft always prevails. Jean and Louis have landed in *Gourmet* magazine, Antonio and Jean cooked for Pavarotti, and Roland Mesnier, a chef who worked with Jean Lafont at the Savoy Hotel in London, served as a chef at the White House. Their stories are filled with culinary wonder and enchantment, the kind you find in travel journals and Proust manuscripts.

The party turned into a beautiful afternoon spent under shady oak trees, playing pétanque, drinking Pernod, telling stories, and amicably competing. The rule of pétanque is to get your steel ball as close to the small wooden ball, the *cochonnet,* as possible. You are of course expected to knock competitors' steel balls out of the way. Jean and Lucette, another French guest, are competing as if this were a tennis match. Tempers ebb and flow, but no matter the outcome of the game, there is always a nice glass of Pernod handy to soothe their egos and parch their thirst.

Cherif's Pastis

Cherif's Pastis

When people envision French drinks, they think of champagne and wine, but in the south of France, pastis such as Pernod is as much a cultural staple as wine. Following are a few of our favorite recipes, best enjoyed with a game of pétanque on a warm summer afternoon. This first recipe is the classic way of serving Pernod.

Yields 2 drinks

Crushed ice
4 tablespoons Pernod
8 tablespoons water

Fill 2 glasses one-third full with crushed ice.

Pour 2 tablespoons Pernod and 4 tablespoons water in each glass. Stir and serve.

Grenadine Pastis

Grenadine Pastis

This pastis is fruity and pink because of the grenadine syrup. It would be the perfect libation for a cocktail party. Don't let the aniseed taste fool you. . . . Pastis has a 40 percent alcohol content.

Yields 2 drinks

Crushed ice
2 tablespoons grenadine syrup
4 tablespoons Pernod
8 tablespoons water

Fill 2 glasses one-third full with crushed ice.

Pour 1 tablespoon grenadine, 2 tablespoons Pernod, and 4 tablespoons water in each glass. Stir and serve.

Death in the Afternoon

Death in the Afternoon

This was author Ernest Hemingway's favorite libation. His version had absinthe with champagne. We gave it a new twist with pastis.

Yields 2 drinks

4 tablespoons Pernod
1½ cups champagne, chilled

In each of 2 champagne glasses, pour 2 tablespoons Pernod and ¾ cup champagne. Stir and serve.

Roasted Leg of Lamb with Sicilian Marinade

Roasted Leg of Lamb with Sicilian Marinade

This is a wonderful recipe when entertaining friends and family.

Yields 8 servings

½ cup olive oil
Juice of 1 large lemon
Salt to taste
Pepper to taste
½ cup assorted fresh herbs (basil, mint, oregano, thyme, Italian parsley, rosemary)
2 large cloves garlic, minced
1 leg of lamb (5-7 pounds), boned and trimmed

Whisk together the olive oil, lemon juice, salt, and pepper.

Chop assorted herbs and add to the olive oil mixture.

Add the garlic.

Pour olive oil mixture over the lamb leg in a roasting pan and allow to marinate for at least 1 hour.

Heat oven to 425 degrees.

Roast lamb for about 20 minutes.

Reduce heat to 300 degrees, and roast lamb for 1 additional hour, until the internal temperature of the lamb reads 135 degrees and it is still pink inside.

Allow the lamb to cool for 10 minutes before slicing.

Beef Volcano

Beef Volcano

The Beef Volcano is Cherif's creative interpretation of the classic dish, boeuf bourguignon. He sculpts a "volcano" of mashed potatoes (see following recipe), inserting the boeuf bourguignon and letting the sauce drip as "lava." Cherif uses beef tenderloin, because the quality is far superior to other stew-type beef cuts.

Yields 4 servings

1 cup water
10 ounces white pearl onions, peeled
Salt to taste
Pepper to taste
1 tablespoon sugar, divided
4 tablespoons + 1 teaspoon butter, divided
1 pound beef tenderloin
2 tablespoons olive oil
2 tablespoons white flour
2 cups red wine (preferably merlot)
2 cups veal stock
4 ounces bacon, crisped and diced
8 ounces button mushrooms, quartered and sautéed

To caramelize onions, boil water in a small pot. Add onions, salt, pepper, 2 teaspoons sugar, and 1 teaspoon butter. Simmer over medium heat until the onions have absorbed all the water, about 15 minutes. Set aside.

Cut the tenderloin in large rectangles measuring 1½" x 1". Season with salt and pepper. In a large pot over medium heat, sear beef in olive oil for 2-3 minutes. Remove beef from pot and set aside.

In the same pot, make a roux by combining 4 tablespoons butter with flour. Cook over medium heat, stirring, for 2 minutes.

Add the wine, veal stock, and 1 teaspoon sugar, stirring often.

Simmer gently over medium heat, uncovered, for 20-22 minutes.

Add the onions, beef, bacon, and mushrooms. Serve hot in "volcano" of mashed potatoes.

Mashed Potatoes

Mashed Potatoes

These are an ideal accompaniment for any hearty dish, and we love making them part of the Beef Volcano presentation.

Yields 4-6 servings

2 pounds Idaho potatoes, peeled and halved
4 cups water
Salt to taste
4 tablespoons butter
1 cup heavy whipping cream
White pepper to taste

Boil potatoes in a large pot with water and salt for 25 minutes. Put knife through potatoes to check that they are tender. The knife should go through very easily.

Remove pot from heat and drain water.

Add butter.

Mash potatoes with a whip or potato masher.

Add heavy cream and keep stirring with the whip.

Add salt and pepper.

If using for Beef Volcano, sculpt into volcano shape.

French Onion Soup

French Onion Soup

When it is cold outside and you feel like warming up your body and soul, nothing beats a hot onion soup.

Yields 8 servings

3 tablespoons olive oil
8 cups sliced yellow onions
1 bay leaf
2 sprigs thyme
½ cup sherry
8 cups chicken stock
1½ teaspoons beef base
Pepper to taste
1 tablespoon soy sauce
Bread croutons
16 slices imported Swiss cheese
Parmesan, grated

Heat olive oil in a Dutch oven over high heat. Add onions and stir for about 15-20 minutes until golden brown. Add bay leaf, thyme, sherry, chicken stock, beef base, pepper, and soy sauce.

Bring to a boil. Reduce heat to medium and simmer for 30-40 minutes.

Set oven broiler to high.

Pour soup into 8 individual ramekins, filling to top. Add croutons on top to cover, about 4 each. Layer 2 slices Swiss cheese on top of each ramekin.

Sprinkle Parmesan on top of Swiss cheese.

Place under broiler for 1-2 minutes.

Mazatlan Pasta Salad

Mazatlan Pasta Salad

This is a colorful and flavorful summer dish. You can adapt it according to your preference by adding chicken or salmon.

Yields 4-6 servings

1 cup olive oil
¼ cup lemon juice
1 cup cilantro
2 jalapenos, seeded and diced
Salt to taste
White pepper to taste
2 avocados, diced
1 pound penne pasta, cooked, drained, and cooled
2 Roma tomatoes, diced
½ cup toasted pumpkin seeds

In a blender, combine olive oil, lemon juice, cilantro, jalapenos, salt, and pepper until smooth.

Add avocados and blend until no chunks remain.

Pour Mazatlan sauce into a bowl. Toss in pasta and chill, covered, in refrigerator.

Serve chilled, garnished with tomatoes and pumpkin seeds.

Heirloom Tomato Salad

Heirloom Tomato Salad

This tomato salad showcases beautiful colors and seasonal ingredients.

Yields 2-4 servings

1½ pounds heirloom tomatoes, quartered
1 can (14 ounces) hearts of palm, drained and sliced
1 large leek, white parts only, thinly sliced
2 ounces arugula, chopped
4 sprigs fresh oregano, leaves only, chopped

In a large bowl, combine tomatoes, hearts of palm, leek, arugula, and oregano.

VINAIGRETTE

4 tablespoons good olive oil
2 tablespoons red wine vinegar
Salt to taste
Pepper to taste

For the vinaigrette, in a separate small bowl, whisk together the olive oil, vinegar, salt, and pepper.

Pour the vinaigrette on top of salad, and toss.

Baked Alaska

Baked Alaska

This show-stopping dessert is easy to make and can be made a day ahead of time. Baked Alaska, also known as a Norwegian omelet, is a cake filled with ice cream and covered with meringue. The sponge cake recipe is adapted from the "father of modern French cuisine" Fernand Point's own recipe. Thomas Jefferson served a dish similar to baked Alaska at one of his banquet dinners during his presidency in 1802.

Yields 8-10 servings

1 pound almonds, roasted
10 ounces skinless hazelnuts, roasted
2 cups sugar, divided
28 egg whites, divided
1 pint vanilla ice cream, softened
1 pint raspberry ice cream, softened
1 pint chocolate ice cream, softened
Maraschino cherries
¼ cup Grand Marnier

Preheat oven to 375 degrees.

For the sponge cake, combine the almonds, hazelnuts, and 1 cup sugar in a food processor.

Whip 16 egg whites to peaks in the bowl of an electric mixer. Fold nut mixture in with a spatula.

Pour mixture into a 17x12" jelly-roll pan lined with wax paper. Bake for about 20-25 minutes. Remove from oven and let cool.

Cut sponge cake to the size of a loaf pan. You should have 2 long sides, 2 short sides, 1 long bottom, and 1 long top to encase the Alaska. Line the bottom and sides of the loaf pan with the appropriate sponge cake pieces.

Spread vanilla ice cream over the bottom piece. Repeat with the raspberry and chocolate. Cover with the top piece of sponge cake. Place in the freezer to harden.

For the meringue, in the bowl of an electric mixer, combine 1 cup sugar and 12 egg whites. Beat to soft peaks. Set aside 1 eggshell.

Remove the sponge cake from the loaf pan. Using a spatula and a pastry bag for decorating, coat sponge cake with meringue. Decorate further with cherries. Place eggshell on top.

Bake the Alaska for 3-4 minutes, watching for color on tips of meringue. Remove from oven.

Pour Grand Marnier inside the warmed eggshell. Light the eggshell.

Tip: If you do not feel comfortable flaming the Alaska, your guests will still be just as impressed with the baked Alaska on its own.

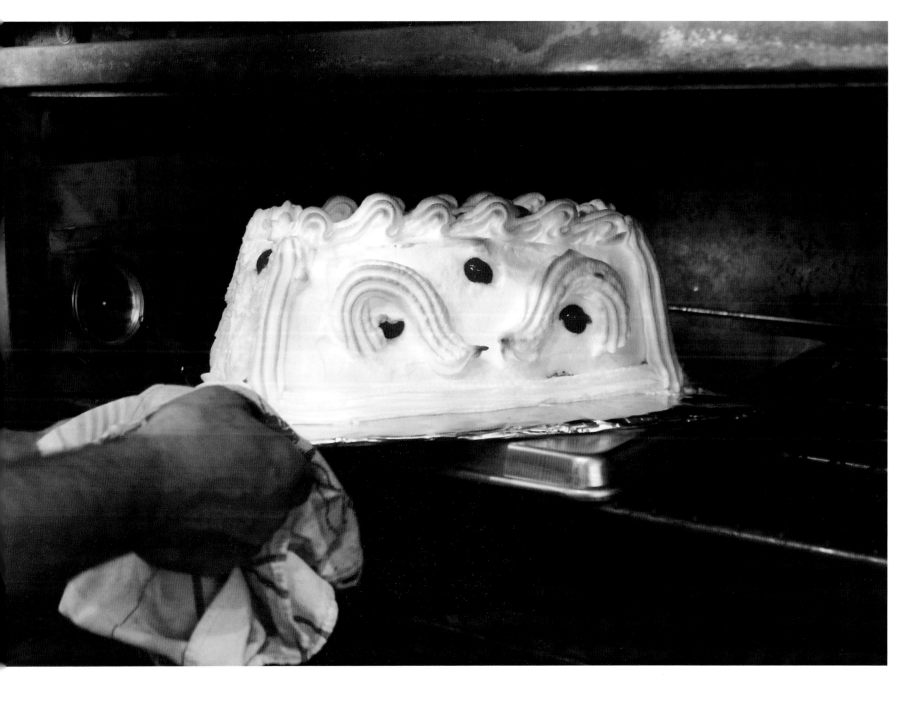

*Cherif, Hedda, and Barbara Bush at Global Health
Corps Day on Hedda's farm*

10

Global Health Corps Day

In 2008, Barbara Bush, daughter of Pres. George W. Bush, founded Global Health Corps with the goal of facilitating local communities' access to health care. The GHC recruits "fellows" from universities to help end disparities in health care through leadership and community development. They receive their training from Stanford University, and each fellow contributes a different set of skills to this cause.

As part of a fundraiser for the health organization, a day at Singletree farm was auctioned off. With Cherif in the kitchen and Hedda hosting, the winner of the auction was treated to a delectable and exciting celebration.

With a successful fundraiser campaign in Dallas for her organization, Ms. Bush was able to send three more fellows to work with one of their partner organizations, to fulfill specific needs for health equity. The GHC has already achieved significant success, sending twenty-two fellows out in the field in East Africa and the United States. Ms. Bush looks forward to the impact her fellows will have on global health-care needs.

Guests arrive at Singletree

Resources

Singletree farm is available for private events. For further information, please visit our Web site: www.risesouffle.com.

For further information about the items featured in the book, please visit www.risesouffle.com, and for antique items, please visit www.antiqueharvest.com.

Hedda's mother, Andrée Gioia, and sister Germaine Gioia

Notes

Chapter 2

1. *Tournebroche:* Roasting spit.

2. Giuseppe Arcimboldo: Sixteenth-century Italian artist known for his arrangements of fruits, flowers, and vegetables into human facelike portraits.

Chapter 3

1. Timbales: The first soufflés were recorded as *timbales* or *tourtes.*

2. Entremet: An old French word meaning "between servings." This word is used to describe a small dish served between courses.

3. Omelette soufflé: Contains Mornay base or pastry cream. It is shaped like an omelette and not prepared in a ramekin; it is served in a platter.

Chapter 4

1. Madeleine: a French sponge cake shaped like a long scallop shell.

2. In *Remembrance of Things Past*, Marcel Proust wrote: I raised to my lips a spoonful of the tea in which I had soaked a morsel of the cake. No sooner had the warm liquid mixed with the crumbs touched my palate than a shudder ran through me and I stopped, intent upon the extraordinary thing that was happening to me. An exquisite pleasure had invaded my senses, something isolated, detached, with no suggestion of its origin. And at once the vicissitudes of life had become indifferent to me, its disasters innocuous, its brevity illusory—this new sensation having had on me the effect which love has of filling me with a precious essence; or rather this essence was not in me it *was* me. I had ceased now to feel mediocre, contingent, mortal. . . . And suddenly the memory revealed itself. The taste was that of the little piece of madeleine which on Sunday mornings at Combray (because on those mornings I did not go out before mass), when I went to say good morning to her in her bedroom, my aunt Léonie used to give me, dipping it first in her own cup of tea or tisane. The sight of the little madeleine had recalled nothing to my mind before I tasted it; perhaps because I had so often seen such things in the meantime, without tasting them, on the trays in pastry-cooks' windows, that their image had dissociated itself from those Combray days to take its place among others more recent; perhaps because of those memories, so long abandoned and put out of mind, nothing now survived, everything was scattered; the shapes of things, including that of the little scallop-shell of pastry, so richly sensual under its severe, religious folds, were either obliterated or had been so long dormant as to have lost the power of expansion which would have allowed them to resume their place in my consciousness. But when from a long-distant past nothing subsists, after the people are dead, after the things are broken and scattered, taste and smell alone, more fragile but more enduring, more unsubstantial, more persistent, more faithful, remain poised a long time, like souls, remembering, waiting, hoping, amid the ruins of all the rest; and bear unflinchingly, in the tiny and almost impalpable drop of their essence, the vast structure of recollection.

3. *Cornichons:* Small pickles.

4. *Tagine:* A North African serving dish with a conical top with an opening and a platelike bottom.

Chapter 5

1. *Relais routier:* Sometimes referred to as a "transport café,"

serving traditional French food along the road for motorists.

2. *Gratin dauphinois:* A potato gratin with cream, garlic, and cheese.

3. *Moules marinières:* A French dish made with mussels, shallots, parsley, and a white wine broth.

4. Val D'Isere: A ski station in the Savoie department of the Rhône-Alpes region in France.

5. *Poularde en vessie:* A chicken cooked inside a pig's bladder.

6. Foie gras: A delicate French "spread" made from the liver of a fattened goose or duck.

7. *Chocolat chaud:* Hot chocolate.

8. *Manoir:* Manor or country house.

Chapter 6

1. Raison d'être: French expression meaning "reason for being."

Chapter 9

1. D'Artagnan: The protagonist in Alexandre Dumas's novel *The Three Musketeers*.

Recipe Index